Emily Post on Etiquette

Also in this series

Emily Post on Entertaining

Emily Post on Weddings

EMILY POST

on

Etiquette

Elizabeth L. Post

Harper Perennial
A Division of HarperCollins Publishers

HarperCollins books may be purchased for educational,
business, or sales promotional use. For information, please
write to: Special Markets Department, HarperCollins
Publishers, Inc., 10 East 53rd Street, New York, N.Y. 10022.

Designed by Kim Llewellyn

Library of Congress Cataloging-in-Publication Data
Post, Emily, 1873–1960.
  Emily Post on etiquette.
  "Perennial Library."
  Includes index.
  ISBN 0-06-080813-6 (pbk.)
  1. Etiquette.   I. Post, Elizabeth L. II. Title.
III. Title: Etiquette.
BJ1853.P6   1987   395   83-48375

ISBN 0-06-274003-2 (pbk.)
94 95 OPM 6 5

Contents

Introduction ix

Everyday Manners 1

Dining In & Dining Out 18

Getting Along with Others 53

Telephone Manners 60

In Houses of Worship 65

At Times of Loss & Grieving 68

Communications 79

Gifts & Giving 90

Tipping 94

Names & Titles on the Job 110

Business Entertaining 112

Being Entertained at Home 115

Invitations & Replies 122

Celebrations 134

Index 151

Introduction

Society's ways and means have changed so dramatically over the past few decades that the rules and guidelines of etiquette have changed too. There are simply more people, so getting along with others can be more difficult than it was before. Whether apartment or backyard neighbors, practicing courtesies is increasingly important. The impact of a discourteous neighbor can be greater than it was in a less populated time because we tend to live closer together.

There are more of us in the work force than ever before too, with a general tendency toward less formality and subsequent confusion as to how to address one another and the rights and wrongs of socializing with and entertaining business associates.

Manners are sometimes based on safety. At-home good telephone manners of yesteryear have become unwise today; the chapter on telephone manners updates what to say and how to say it, so you can better protect yourself and your family.

As we come of age and expand the number of people we know socially and through business, we are faced with difficult times of loss and grieving. As with so many other aspects of etiquette, the guidelines help us get through these times and give us the ways to know what to do and to be of assistance to others.

Good manners have always been based on common sense and thoughtfulness, and that hasn't changed. New situations, however, often give us experiences we have not faced before. This book has been designed to answer the questions these situations present, whether host, guest, manager, employee, traveler, invitee, or invitor. Included are the up-to-the-minute answers to the questions I am asked most often by men and women alike. From everyday good manners to special celebrations, there are times when our instincts tell us what to do, but there are other times when we just aren't sure. This book is arranged in such a way that it is easy to reference your question and find the most current solution to new-decade etiquette dilemmas. When times are so rushed, it is very nice to have ways to smooth the paths between people and establish pleasant relationships. Think of etiquette not as a strict set of rules, but as a code of behavior, based on kindness and consideration. Manners are the tools that help us live by that code.

Everyday Manners

Q. *What are the rules for making introductions? Are there forms that should be avoided?*

A. The overall rule is that one person is always introduced to another. This is achieved either by the actual use of the word *to*—"Mr. Welch, I'd like to introduce you to Mr. Arthur"—or by saying the name of the person to whom the other is being introduced first, without using the preposition *to*. An example of this is: "Mrs. Andreas, may I introduce Mr. Hearne."

In addition to the overall rule, there are three basic rules:

1. A man is always introduced *to* a woman.
   "Mrs. Griffiths, I'd like you to meet Mr. Jardine."
   "Jill, this is my cousin, John Marshall."
   "Mr. Wilcox, may I introduce you *to* my mother, Mrs. Boothby."

2. A young person is always introduced *to* an older person.
   "Dr. Stanhope, I'd like you to meet my daughter, Lily Schumann."
   "Aunt Lorraine, this is my roommate, Gianetta Donegan."

3. A less important person is always introduced *to* a more important person. This rule can be complicated, since it may be difficult to determine who is more important. There is one guideline which may help in some circumstances: Members of your family, even though they may be more prominent, are introduced *to* the other person as a matter of courtesy.

"Mr. Conover, I'd like you to meet my stepfather, Governor Heard."

"Mrs. Jamison, this is my aunt, Professor Myers."

The easiest way not to slip up is to always say the name of the woman, the older person, or the more prominent person first, followed by the phrase, "I'd like you to meet . . . " or "this is . . . " or "may I introduce . . . ". If you inadvertently say the wrong name first, correct your slip by saying, "Mr. Heath, I'd like to introduce you to Mrs. McGregor."

Yes, there are forms to be avoided:

Don't introduce people by their first names only. Always include a person's full name.

When phrasing your introduction, avoid expressing it as a command, such as "Mr. Bonner, shake hands with Mr. Heath," or "Mrs. Digby, meet my cousin, Barbara."

Avoid calling only one person "my friend" in an introduction. It implies that the other person isn't your friend.

When you introduce yourself, don't begin by saying, "What's your name?" Start by giving your own name: "Hello, I'm Joan Hamburg . . . "

Do not repeat "Mr. Jones . . . Mr. Smith. Mr. Smith . . . Mr. Jones." To say each name once is enough.

Do not refer to your spouse as "Mr. Jansen" or "Mrs. J." in conversation. Rather, refer to him or her as "my husband" or "my wife" in situations where first names are not being used.

Q. *Are there occasions when first names aren't used? What are they?*
A. Yes, there are. When meeting someone in the following categories, first names may not be used except by specific request:

- A superior in one's business
- A business client or customer
- A person of higher rank (a diplomat, a public official, a professor, for example)
- Professional people offering you their services (doctors, lawyers, etc.). In turn, they should not use your first name unless you request them to.
- An older person

Q. *Is it necessary to specify my relationship to someone when introducing family members?*
A. No, it is not necessary, but it is helpful to include an identifying phrase. This provides a conversational opening for strangers. Since you courteously give

precedence to the other person when introducing a
family member, the identifying phrase comes at the
end of the introduction: "Mrs. Cottrell, I'd like you to
meet my daughter, Deborah."

Q. *How do you introduce your live-in partner?*
A. Although you usually identify family members as
such, you needn't identify boyfriends, girlfriends, or
live-in companions with their relationship to you. Saying his or her name is sufficient.

Q. *Should children introduce their parents by using
first names?*
A. It depends upon to whom they are making the
introduction. One should always use the name that
the newly introduced pair will use in talking to each
other. If you are introducing your roommate to your
father, he would, of course, call your father by the
title "Mr." If you are introducing your roommate's
father to your father, you would use your father's
full name: "Mr. Davies, may I introduce my father,
Franklin Palmer."

Q. *How should stepparents be introduced?*
A. There is nothing derogatory or objectionable in
the terms *stepmother* or *stepfather,* and the simplest form
of introduction, said in the warmest tone to indicate
an affectionate relationship, is: "Mrs. Hibbing, I'd like
you to meet my stepfather, Mr. Brown." Even if you
call your stepfather by his first name, he should be
introduced to your peers or younger persons as "Mr.
Brown," not "Jack."

Q. *What should a newlywed call his or her spouse's parents?*

A. There is no definite answer to this question. The choice of names is purely personal. The parents, simply because they are older, should take the initiative and suggest a name that their new daughter-in-law or son-in-law should call them if there is awkwardness or if he or she is still calling them "Mr. and Mrs." If the parents do not make the first move, it is perfectly all right to ask them what they'd like to be called, since "Mr. and Mrs." sounds too formal.

Q. *What names should children use when addressing their parents' friends?*

A. They should call them "Mr." or "Mrs." unless their parents' friends have requested that they call them by their first names or by nicknames.

Q. *How should ex-family members be introduced?*

A. If the introduction is very casual and it is not likely that any of the people involved will see each other again, no explanation is necessary. If the new acquaintanceship is likely to continue, it is important to explain the relationship as clearly as possible. A former mother-in-law would say, "I'd like you to meet Mary Dunbar. Mary is John's (or my son's) widow and is now married to Joe Dunbar." Had Mary been divorced, the mother-in-law would say, "Mary was John's wife and is now married to . . ." Mary's introduction of her former mother-in-law will be, "This is Mrs. Judson, Sarah's grandmother," or "my first husband's mother."

Q. *How do you address correspondence to a married couple who use different surnames? Would the form of address differ if they were not married?*

A. Correspondence to a married couple with different names should be addressed so that both names appear on the same line:

Mr. Jonathan Adams and Ms. Angela Blake

If the couple is unmarried, the names should be on separate lines:

Ms. Susan Amber
Mr. Howard Cole

Q. *How should a married woman sign letters, with her business name or married name? Does it matter if the letter is for business or social purposes?*

A. If a woman has continued to use her maiden name in business after marriage, she would sign correspondence with the name she is known by professionally, or her maiden name. Her personal correspondence would be signed with her married name, since it is likely that is how she is known socially or in her community.

If a woman has legally retained her maiden name at marriage, all correspondence, whether business or social, would be signed with her maiden name, which is her legal name.

Q. *Does a married woman's name differ from the form a widow uses?*

A. No, a woman who is currently married and a

widow generally use the same form, "Mrs. James Scott." A widow may use her first name if she wishes, but in that case she may be mistaken for a divorcée, and most older women prefer to continue using their husband's name.

Q. *What name does a divorcée use?*
A. A divorcée does not continue to use her husband's first name and is addressed as Mrs. Celia Dwyer, not Mrs. Philip Dwyer.

Q. *How are professional women addressed in social situations?*
A. A woman who is a medical doctor, a dentist, etc., is addressed by, and introduced with, her title, socially as well as professionally.

Q. *My husband is named after his father and uses the suffix "Jr." after his name. We are naming our son after my husband's uncle. Do we attach a suffix after his name, and if so, would it also be "Jr."?*
A. Yes, he may receive a suffix after his name, but a child named after his grandfather (whose name is different than the child's father's), uncle, or cousin is called "2nd," not "Jr." Were your son to be named after his father, who is named after his own father, the suffix would be "3rd."

Q. *My family has chosen to shorten our very long surname to a more manageable one. How can we let everyone know we've done this?*
A. The quickest and simplest way is to send out formal announcements:

Mr. and Mrs. Brian Malinowsky
Announce that by Permission of the Court
They and Their Children
Have Taken the Family Name of
Malin

Q. *I often forget people's names and am at a loss to introduce them to others. How can I make introductions under these situations?*
A. There is nothing you can do but introduce the friend who has joined you to the person whose name you've forgotten by saying to the latter, "Oh, do you know Janet McCall?"

Hopefully the nameless person will be tactful and understanding enough to announce his own name. If he doesn't, and your friend makes matters worse by saying, "You didn't tell me *his* name," it's even more embarrassing. The only solution is to be completely frank, admit you're having a mental block, and ask them to complete the introduction themselves.

Remember the feeling, however, and when you meet someone who obviously doesn't remember your name, or might not remember it, offer it at once. Say immediately, "Hello, I'm Julie Hopewell, I met you at the Anderson's last Christmas." Never say, "You don't remember me, do you?" which embarrasses the other person and puts him or her on the defensive.

Q. *What can I say when introduced besides "how do you do?"*
A. Whether you say "how do you do" or "hello"

when introduced to another, follow with the person's name, which adds respect and helps commit the name to memory. Your tone of voice indicates degrees of warmth, and if you are introduced to someone you have wanted to meet, you can follow "How do you do, Mr. Struthers" or "Hello, Mrs. Jenson" with "I'm so glad to meet you—Jerry Ernst speaks of you all the time!" or whatever may be the reason for your special interest. If you are introduced and left standing with the person you've just met, of course you would attempt further conversation. A positive comment on the occasion, the food, or even the weather are all safe and noncontroversial openers.

Q. *How do I correct my host or hostess when I've been incorrectly introduced?*
A. It is only sensible and kind to correct the error immediately, but not with annoyance. If possible, make light of it so as not to embarrass the host or hostess. All you need say is, "I know it's confusing, but my name is Light, not Bright," or "Just so you can find me in the phone book, I'm June Smith, not Jane Smith."

Q. *I never know whether or not to shake hands. Are there any guidelines to help me judge this situation?*
A. Yes, there are guidelines, but they are flexible and if someone is not aware of them, the guidelines should be overlooked and the proper response made.

For example, strictly speaking, it is a woman's place to offer her hand or not to a man, but if he should extend his hand first, she must give him hers.

Technically, it is the place of a man to whom another is being introduced to offer his hand first, but the gesture is usually simultaneous.

Adults offer their hands to children first. Really, the guidelines for shaking hands follow the guidelines for introductions: A woman offers her hand first; an older person initiates a handshake with a younger one; and the more important person, or the one to whom someone is being introduced, is the first to offer his or her hand.

Q. *Under what circumstances does a man rise when introduced to a woman? Do women stand when being introduced? Does it matter if the situation is social or for business?*

A. A man should rise when a woman comes into a room for the first time and remain standing until she is seated or leaves the vicinity, or unless she says, "Thank you, but please sit down, I'm leaving in just a moment," or words to that effect. He does not jump up and down every time a hostess or another guest goes in and out.

When a client, whether woman or man, goes to a man's office on business, he should stand up and receive him or her, offer a chair, and not sit down until after the client is seated. When the client rises to leave he stands, escorts the client to the door, and holds the door for him or her. Neither a man nor a woman rises for a secretary or co-worker in the office.

A woman receiving a male client in her office may remain seated, but generally follows the same guidelines as given above for a man receiving clients in his office. She would definitely rise for a much older woman.

In a restaurant, when a woman greets a man in passing, he merely makes the gesture of rising slightly from his chair and nodding. If she pauses to speak for a moment, he rises fully and introduces her to others at his table.

Both the host and hostess always rise to greet each arriving guest. Members of the host's family, including young people, also rise as a guest enters the room, with the exception of a child who is sitting and chatting with an adult. He or she may continue the conversation, seated, unless the guest is brought over to be introduced, in which case the child should stand up instantly.

A woman does not stand when being introduced to someone at a distance, nor need she rise when shaking hands with anyone, unless the person is much older, very prominent, or is someone with whom she wants to go on talking. A woman should not jump to her feet for a woman who is only a few years older than she, since rising indicates, among other things, respect for age. The gesture, although well meant, would more than likely not be well received.

Q. *When walking down the street are men expected to walk closest to the curb or to the buildings?*
A. It used to be that men always walked between a woman and the street to protect her from runaway or obstreperous horses and splashing mud from carriage

wheels on unpaved roads. Although this need rarely exists today, the pattern of the men walking curbside has been established and still is followed. If a man chooses to ignore the curbside rule, he should always walk on the woman's left.

Q. *Does the "ladies first" rule always apply?*
A. In most circumstances, indoors or out, when a couple walks together, the woman precedes the man. There are times, however, when a man goes first:

> Over rough ground, he walks beside her and offers his hand if she needs assistance.

> He steps ahead of her to open a car door when she enters it.

> He gets out first and holds the door for her when they arrive, unless she doesn't want to wait.

> He precedes her down a steep or slippery stairway. However, he follows her up or down an escalator unless she asks him to go first to help her on or off.

> He makes the gesture of stepping into a boat first, or off a bus first, to be ready to help her, unless she prefers that he not do so.

> He steps into a revolving door that is not already moving ahead of a woman, but she precedes him through one that is already moving.

Q. *Are men still expected to give up their seats for women on trains and buses? What about children giving up seats to adults?*
A. A man is not expected to give up his seat unless

a woman is elderly, infirm, pregnant, or burdened with a baby or a heavy armful of any sort. Otherwise it is to be assumed that a man who has worked all day is just as tired as the women on the train or bus. Of course a man may offer his seat to any woman if he wishes, and she may accept or refuse his offer as she wishes.

Children, on the other hand, should be taught to offer their seats to older people, both men and women. Generally, youngsters are strong, they have not usually worked as hard, and furthermore, it is a gesture of courtesy and respect.

Q. *Who gets off the elevator first, men or women?*
A. In a crowded elevator, whoever is nearest the door gets off first, whether men or women. In elevators that are not crowded or apartment or private elevators, a woman precedes a man out the door, just as she would in any room in a house.

Q. *Should a couple walk hand in hand down a crowded street? Are there any acceptable public displays of affection?*
A. There is nothing wrong with walking hand in hand in public, unless doing so causes pedestrian traffic to be impeded. In this case, single file is the rule until the sidewalk is less crowded. The only acceptable forms of public displays of affection are holding hands and casual or affectionate kisses or hugs when greeting an old friend. Other physical displays of affection should take place in private.

Q. *There seem to be fewer and fewer cigarette smokers these days. How does a smoker know when and where it is okay to have a cigarette?*
A. If a smoker is in a home not visited before or with people he or she doesn't know, or in close proximity to other people, the smoker should ask, "Do you mind if I smoke?"

If they do, don't smoke. It's also important to keep in mind the places one absolutely must not smoke:

- In a church, synagogue, or during any religious service or proceeding
- In a home sickroom or hospital room
- In a doctor's waiting room or other waiting room when others are present
- When dancing
- On buses and nonsmoking sections of trains and planes
- In museums and galleries
- Inside theaters
- Inside all department stores and most smaller stores
- In proximity to infants or small children

Every year, new no-smoking laws are passed, many on a local basis. One should always consider these ordinances and when not sure, ask.

Q. *Can you offer any guidelines for apartment living?*
A. The best guideline, as with many rules of etiquette, is the consideration of others. Don't do things

you wouldn't want done to you. Don't deface property, litter, allow garbage to build up, or be insensitive
about noise. Children's play may not seem loud, nor
does the radio, stereo, or television set when you're
in the same room with them, but those sounds carry
easily from one apartment to another. Although some
noise is to be expected, it is not to be expected at the
crack of dawn or late at night. At these times, noise-
making should be eliminated. At others, if the decibel
level is very high with dogs barking, children scream-
ing, or babies crying, sounds should be softened as
much as possible by shutting windows temporarily.

Q. *How should people behave at parks and playgrounds? At public beaches?*
A. People should behave in public as they would in
their own homes or yards, by cleaning up after themselves, not by behaving as though there was a hired
staff to follow behind and restore to order what they
destroy.

At the beach, there are additional considerations:

Avoid crowding. Don't choose a spot right next
to someone already there.

If you have children in tow, choose a spot close
to where they will play so they don't need to
run past other people to get there and back,
splashing water and kicking sand.

Loud radios and tape players are an intrusion on
others. Wear earphones, or keep the volume so
low only you can hear it.

Public displays of affection are distasteful and especially uncomfortable for people with children. Save physical contact for private.

Practice good taste in beach apparel. Unless you are specifically at a private beach, keep your swimming attire up, on, and fastened, as well as appropriate to your figure type and body weight.

The guidelines for behavior at parks and playgrounds are the same as for beaches. In addition:

Don't spread your picnic baskets and personal belongings over two or three tables when your share is one. Offer to share a table if you don't need the whole space.

Be polite. Although table manners needn't be formal, they also shouldn't be offensive to others who can't help seeing them.

Help children share and take turns on play equipment.

Leave public grounds cleaner than you found them. If everyone cleaned up his own mess plus one item more, our countryside would soon regain the beauty it has in many places lost.

Q. *When visiting the home of friends who own pets can I, without appearing rude, protest their dog's jumping on me or their cat's sitting on my lap?*
A. Yes. If it really bothers you, remain pleasant and

ask that the animal be put in another room. Simply say, "I'm sorry, but cats (or dogs) really bother me—would you mind removing Tabby (or Fido) from the room until I leave?"

A good host or hostess will automatically keep animals away when visitors are new acquaintances, to make sure their cat or dog doesn't bother the guest. Even though the host and hostess are quite used to their pet's jumping into laps, etc., guests are not and there is no need to force the presence of animals who are not perfectly behaved on them.

Dining In
& Dining Out

Q. *What is the primary rule governing table manners? Can you suggest any "do's" and "don't's" for dining?*

A. Consideration for others is the rule governing good table manners. To let anyone see what you have in your mouth is offensive. To make "eating" noises is repulsive. To make a mess is disgusting. To saw away at one's meat with elbows high is to risk poking one's neighbor. To scrape or drag chairs, rattle knives and forks against the plate, or make other unnecessary noises is thoroughly annoying to those nearby. Avoiding these poor habits make eating pleasant for all. In addition, there are other "don't's" that, when eliminated, create good table manners:

> Don't encircle your plate with your arm.
>
> Don't push your plate back when finished.
>
> Don't lean back and announce "I'm through" or "I'm stuffed." Putting your utensils down across your plate shows that you have finished.
>
> Don't put liquid in your mouth if it is already filled with food.

Don't crook your finger when picking up a cup or glass. It's an affected mannerism.

Don't ever leave your spoon in your cup or in a stemmed glass.

Don't cut up your entire meal before you start to eat. Cut only one or two bites at a time.

Don't take huge mouthfuls of anything.

Don't leave half the food on your spoon or fork. Learn to put less on and then eat it in one bite.

Don't, if you are a woman, wear an excessive amount of lipstick to the table. Not only can it stain napkins, but it also looks unattractive on the rims of cups and glasses or on the silver.

Don't wipe off the tableware in a restaurant. If your silver is dirty, ask the waiter or waitress for a clean replacement.

Q. *When dining "family style" do you use the same table manners as when dining in a restaurant?*
A. Yes, you use the same table manners, although the environment is not as formal. The dining table, by necessity, is often in a dining ell or the kitchen. A pretty cloth or place mats should be used. A centerpiece, although not necessary, is pleasing, and can be arranged by children, to give them a way to participate and to recognize the importance of household appointments.

Q. *Does the table setting for a family dinner differ from the table setting when guests join the family for dinner?*
A. The main difference between a table setting for guests and a table setting for family is that for the latter a minimum of utensils and plates is put at each place setting. Butter plates and knives are often omitted for family dinners, and the bread and butter are placed at the edge of the dinner plate, for example. What is important is that good manners are practiced, as well as graciousness and consideration for others at the table.

Q. *What is the proper way to sit at a dinner table?*
A. Ideal posture is to sit straight, but not stiffly, against the back of the chair. Hands, when one is not actually eating, may be in the lap. Tipping one's chair is unforgivable.

Q. *How is the table set for . . .*
. . . a formal meal?
A. There is only one rule for a formal table and that is that everything must be geometrically spaced—the centerpiece in the actual center, the places at equal distances, and all utensils balanced.

A formal place setting consists of:

- Service plate, positioned so the pattern "picture" faces the diner
- Butter plate, placed above the forks at the left of the place setting

Formal dinner table

- Wineglasses, positioned according to size
- Salad fork, placed directly to the left of the plate, assuming salad is served with or after the entrée
- Meat fork, positioned to the left of the salad fork
- Fish fork, positioned to the left of the meat fork. Since it is used first, it is to the outside left.
- Salad knife, just to the right of the plate

- Meat knife, placed to the right of the salad knife
- Fish knife, positioned to the right of the meat knife
- Butter knife, positioned diagonally at the top of the butter plate
- Soup spoon and/or fruit spoon placed outside the knives
- Oyster fork, if shellfish is to be served, beyond the spoons. This is the only fork ever placed on the right.
- Napkin

No more than three of any one implement are ever placed on the table (with the exception of the use

Formal place setting

of an oyster fork making four forks). If more than three courses are served before dessert, therefore, the fork for the fourth course is brought in with the course; or the salad fork and knife may be omitted in the beginning and brought in when salad is served.

Dessert spoons and forks are brought in on the dessert plate just before dessert is served.

Q. . . . *a less formal meal?*
A. As at a formal dinner, everything on the table should be symmetrically and evenly spaced. Otherwise, you have much more latitude in planning an informal, casual, or semiformal dinner than you do for a formal dinner. You may use color in your table linens or other table appointments. Candles are used, just as they are on formal dinner tables, but usually as single candles rather than candelabra. They may be of any color that complements your table setting, but they must be high or low enough so that the flame is not at the eye level of the diners.

For an informal place setting, there is less of everything. There are fewer courses served, so fewer pieces of silver are set out. The typical place setting for an informal, three-course dinner includes:

- Two forks, one for dinner placed at the far left and one for dessert or salad positioned directly to the left of the plate
- Dinner plate, not on the table when guests sit down
- Salad plate, to the left of the forks

Informal table set for six

- Butter plate, placed above the forks
- Dinner knife, next to the plate on the right (for steak, chops, chicken, or game birds it may be a steak knife)

- Butter knife, placed diagonally across the bread plate
- Two spoons, a dessert spoon positioned to the right of the knife and a soup spoon to the right of the dessert spoon
- Water goblet, placed above the knife
- Wineglass, positioned slightly forward of and to the right of the water goblet
- Napkin, placed between the forks and the knife

Service plates are not used at an informal dinner, except in an appropriate size and style under a stemmed glass used for shrimp cocktail, fruit cup, etc., and under soup plates.

The dinner plate should not be on the table when

Informal three-course dinner place setting

you sit down, assuming you wish it to be warm when the food is served.

If you plan to serve coffee with the meal, the cup and saucer go to the right of the setting, with the coffee spoon on the table at the right of or on the saucer.

Q. . . . *a family-style meal?*
A. Practicality is the keynote in setting the table for family meals. A minimum number of utensils is put at each place—only those absolutely necessary. Since there is usually only one course and dessert, there may be only three pieces of silver—a fork, a knife, and a spoon for the dessert. Of course if you are having soup or fruit first, utensils for those foods must be added. It is not necessary to have separate salad forks, although individual salad bowls should be set out.

Frozen dinners should not be eaten from the containers, but should be spooned out onto warm plates.

Ketchup, jellies, pickles, etc., may be served in their jars if no guests are present. The jars should be on saucers, and each should have its own separate serving spoon or fork on the saucer. Paper napkins are perfectly correct for family meals. However, if you prefer cloth napkins, you may wish to conserve on your laundry by using napkin rings. Each family member has his own ring. He folds his napkin at the end of the meal and puts it back in the ring, which is removed from the table until the next meal. Napkins should be changed after two or three meals.

Since no china or silver that will not be used need

Family place setting

be placed on the table, the following setting may be used, according to your menu:

- Dinner fork at the left of the plate
- Dinner knife at the right of the plate, then the soup spoon or the oyster fork or the dessert spoon on the outside
- Glass or goblet for a beverage at the right above the knife
- Butter plate, if used, to the left and above the fork, with the butter knife laid on it diagonally from the upper left to the lower right
- Salad plate at the left of the fork
- Napkin at the left or in the center of the setting

- Coffee mug or cup and saucer with a spoon at the right

If the food is to be passed, the warm dinner plates are at each place on the table when the family sits down, or they are stacked in front of the head of the household if he or she is to serve. Often plates are served directly from the stove in order to avoid the use of extra platters and serving dishes.

Q. *What should a guest do when dining with a family of another faith who say grace before meals, sit quietly or join in?*
A. A guest certainly may join in if he or she feels comfortable doing so. However, it is not necessary for guests to cross themselves, even though their Catholic hosts do so—nor to make any gesture not practiced in their own faith. If a guest chooses not to join in grace, he or she may sit (or stand) quietly until grace is finished. A clue as to whether grace is to be said is whether the hostess immediately puts her napkin in her lap. If she does not, it is a signal that she is waiting to say grace as soon as everyone is silent.

Q. *What is the proper way to handle a napkin at dinner?*
A. Ordinarily, as soon as you are seated you put your napkin in your lap. At a formal dinner, however, you wait for your hostess to put hers on her lap first. Remove the napkin from the table, place it on your lap, and unfold it as much as necessary with both hands. Never tuck it in to your collar, belt, or between but-

tons of a shirt. When using your napkin, blot or pat your lips—never wipe with it as if it were a washcloth.

When the meal is finished, or if you leave the table during the meal, put the napkin on the left side of your place, or if the plates have been removed, in the center. It should not be crumpled up, nor should it be refolded; rather, it is laid on the table in loose folds so that it does not spread itself out. At a dinner party, the hostess lays her napkin on the table as a signal that the meal is over, and the guests then lay their napkins on the table—not before.

Q. *How do I know when to start eating as a guest at dinner?*
A. It is incumbent upon the host or hostess to ask guests to begin a hot course after three or four people have been served. This keeps the food of those who have been served first from getting cold. Although most of us have been raised to wait for the hostess to "lift her fork" before starting, this is true only for a first course and for dessert. For a hot entrée, if she forgets to encourage guests to begin, it is not incorrect for them to start eating after three or four have been served.

Q. *Which glasses are used for which wines? Where are the glasses placed?*
A. Sherry, which is served at room temperature, is poured into small, V-shaped glasses.

White wine, which is served well chilled, is poured into round-bowled, stemmed glasses.

Red wine, which is served at room temperature,

Flute   German   Alsace

Sherry   White wine

Bordeaux   Burgundy

Red wine

Types of wineglasses

is poured into less rounded, more tulip-shaped glasses that are narrower at the rim than are white wine glasses.

Champagne, which is served very well chilled, is poured into either flat, wide-rimmed glasses or into champagne flutes—stemmed glasses that are long and narrow.

Two types of champagne glasses

Wineglasses are placed on the table according to size so that the smaller ones are not hidden behind the larger ones.

The water goblet is placed directly above the knives at the right of the plates.

The champagne glass is next to it at a slight distance to the right.

The claret or red wine glass or the white wine glass is positioned in front of and between the water goblet and champagne glass.

The sherry glass is placed either to the right or in front of the wineglass.

Rather than grouping the wineglasses, you may place them in a straight row slanting downward from the water goblet at the upper left to the sherry glass at the lower right.

Grouped glasses

Glasses in a row

Q. *Is it correct to reach for something—a serving dish, for instance—across the table?*

A. No, it is never correct to reach across the table. It is correct to reach for anything that does not necessitate stretching across your neighbor or leaning far across the table yourself. If the item you want is not close at hand, simply ask the person nearest to it, "Would you please pass the butter, George?"

Q. *May a dinner guest ask the hostess for an item that does not appear on the table, such as mustard when ham is served?*

A. Yes, it is correct if an accompaniment that is ordinarily served is missing, probably because of an oversight. You should not, however, ask for anything unusual that your hostess might not have.

Q. *How should guests serve themselves at a family-style dinner?*

A. Anything served on a piece of toast, with the exception of game birds, should be lifted from the platter on the toast. The toast with its topping is lifted with the spoon and held in place with the fork. If you don't want to eat the toast, simply put it to one side of your plate.

Gravy should be put *on* the meat, potatoes, or rice and condiments at the side of whatever they accompany. Olives, nuts, radishes, or celery are put on the bread-and-butter plate if there is one, otherwise on the edge of the plate from which one is eating.

When a serving dish is passed around the table

for each guest to help himself, it is passed counterclockwise. Each person helps himself and then may offer to hold the dish for the next person.

Q. *May I refuse a dish at dinner I dislike?*
A. If you are among friends, you may refuse with a polite "No, thank you." Otherwise it is good manners to take at least a little of every dish that is offered to you and eat it. You need not give your reason for refusing a dish, but if it is because of an allergy, diet, or other physical cause, you may quietly explain to your hostess without drawing the attention of the entire table. When declining a dish offered by a waiter, say "No, thank you," quietly. At a buffet dinner you need only help yourself to those dishes that appeal to you.

Q. *How do you know with which piece of flatware to begin eating?*
A. It's easy! You always start with the implement of each type that is farthest from the plate. There is only one exception to this rule. If the table is incorrectly set and you realize it, you must choose the implement that is appropriate. For example, if the small shellfish fork has been put next to the plate, you would not use the big dinner fork for the shrimp cocktail and leave the little fork for the entrée, even though they were placed in that order.

Q. *What is the proper way to use a knife and fork?*
A. The American custom of "zigzag" eating (changing the fork from the left to the right hand after cut-

American style of using a knife and fork

ting) is perfectly correct. The knife is put down on the plate after cutting and the fork is raised to the mouth, tines up.

Equally correct is the European method of leaving the fork in the left hand after cutting and raising it to the mouth in the same position in which it was held for cutting, tines down.

The knife may also be used as a "pusher," if necessary. It is held in the left hand in the same position as when cutting with the right hand, and the tip of the blade helps to guide and push the food onto the fork.

When the main course is finished, the knife and fork are placed beside each other on the dinner plate diagonally from upper left to lower right, the handles extended slightly over the edge of the plate. The dessert spoon and/or fork is placed in the same position. If dessert is served in a stemmed or deep bowl on

European style of using a knife and fork

another plate, the dessert spoon is put down on the plate, never left in the bowl. If the bowl is shallow and wide, the spoon may be left in it, or on the plate below it, as you wish.

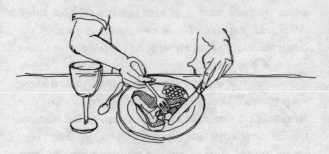

Using knife as a pusher

Q. *How should you . . .*
         . . . eat dessert?

A. Dessert may be eaten with a spoon or fork or both. Stewed fruit is held in place with the fork and cut and eaten with the spoon. Peaches or other juicy fruits are peeled and then eaten with knife and fork, but dry fruits, such as apples, may be cut and then eaten with the fingers.

Pie is eaten with a fork; if it is à la mode, the spoon is also used.

Ice cream is generally eaten with a spoon, but when accompanied by cake, either the spoon alone or both the spoon and fork may be used.

If you cannot eat a dessert—no matter what it is —whether plum, Napoleon, or cream puff—without getting it all over your fingers, you must use a fork and, when necessary, a spoon or a knife also.

Q. *. . . eat soups?*
A. Either clear soup or thick soup may be served in

a cup with one handle or with handles on both sides. After taking a spoonful or two you may pick up the cup if the soup is cool enough, or continue to use your spoon if you prefer.

Clear soups are sometimes served in a shallow soup plate. When the level of the soup is so low that you must tip the plate to avoid scraping the bottom, lift the near edge and tip the plate away from you, never toward you. Spoon the soup either away from you or toward you, whichever is less awkward.

Both soup cups and soup plates should be served with a saucer or a plate beneath them. The spoon, when not in use and when the soup is finished, is laid on the saucer when a soup cup is used, but is left in the soup plate rather than on the plate under it.

Q. . . . *eat bread and butter?*
A. Bread should be broken with the fingers into moderate-sized pieces, not necessarily single-mouthful bits. To butter bread, hold a piece on the edge of the bread-and-butter plate or the place plate. With a butter knife, spread enough butter on it for a mouthful or two at a time. If there is no butter knife, use any other knife you find available, taking care not to smear food particles from the knife onto the butter.

Commonsense exceptions are hot biscuits or toast which can be buttered all over immediately, since they are most delicious when the butter is melted. No bread, however, should be held flat on the palm of the hand and buttered with the hand held in the air!

Q. . . . *eat salad?*

A. If large leaves of lettuce or large chunks of salad vegetables are in the salad, they may be cut with a knife and fork into small, manageable pieces before being eaten. This is preferable to attempting to roll large lettuce leaves around the tines of the fork; if they let go they shoot salad dressing all over you, the table, and your neighbors.

Q. . . . *drink hot beverages?*

A. When hot coffee, chocolate, or tea is served in a mug instead of in a cup and saucer, the problem arises of what to do with the spoon—which should never be left in the mug. The solution depends somewhat on the table covering. If the placemats or tablecloth are paper or plastic, the spoon may be wiped clean with the lips and laid beside the mug. If the mats or cloth are fabric, the bowl of the spoon, face down, should be rested on the edge of the butter plate or dinner plate, with the spoon handle on the table. You may ask for a dish on which to place a tea bag (after pressing out excess liquid against the side of the mug with a spoon) or put it on the edge of the butter or dinner plate.

When hot beverages are served in a cup with a saucer, the spoon is placed at the side of the saucer, as is a tea bag. When the beverage slops into the saucer, the best course is to replace the saucer with a clean one. If this is not possible, rather than drip coffee each time you lift the cup to your mouth, it is permissible to pour the liquid back into the cup and use a paper napkin to dry the bottom of the cup.

Beverages that are too hot to drink may be sipped, never slurped, from a spoon.

Q. . . . *drink iced tea or coffee?*
A. Preferably, iced tea and coffee are served in a glass placed on a saucer or coaster. The saucer, then, is the place to put the iced tea spoon. Otherwise, the spoon may be rested as a spoon served with a mug of coffee or tea, described above.

Q. . . . *use salt in a saltcellar?*
A. If there is no spoon in a saltcellar (a tiny, open bowl), use the tip of a clean knife. If the saltcellar is for you alone, you also may take a pinch with your fingers. Salt that is to be dipped into should be put on the bread-and-butter plate or on the rim of whatever plate is in front of you. Food should be salted only after it has been tasted, never before.

Q. . . . *handle food that is too hot or spoiled?*
A. If a bite of food is too hot, quickly take a swallow of water. Only if there is no beverage at all, and your mouth is scalding, should you spit it out. It should be removed onto your fork or into your fingers and quickly put on the edge of the plate. Spoiled food should not be swallowed but removed as quickly and as unobtrusively as possible, also with fork or fingers. To spit anything whatever into a napkin is unnecessary and not permissible.

Q. *What do you do when . . .*

. . . you begin choking on meat or bones?

A. If a sip of water does not help but a good cough will, cover your mouth with your napkin and cough. Remove the abrasive morsel with your fingers and put it on the edge of your plate. If you continue to cough, excuse yourself from the table. In the event that you are really choking, you will be unable to speak. Don't hesitate to get someone's attention to help you. The seriousness of your condition will quickly be recognized, and it is no time to worry about manners. Keeping calm and acting quickly might well save your life.

Q. *. . . you need to cough, sneeze, or blow your nose?*

A. Cover your mouth and nose with your handkerchief or, if you have no handkerchief, with your napkin. In an emergency, your hand will do better than nothing at all. It is not necessary to leave the table to perform these functions unless the bout turns out to be prolonged. In that case, you should excuse yourself until the seizure has passed. You also should excuse yourself if you have no handkerchief or tissue and need to blow your nose. Never use your napkin to blow your nose.

Q. *. . . discover stones, bugs, or hair in your food?*

A. If it is not too upsetting to you, remove the object without calling attention to it and go on eating. If you are truly repulsed, leave the dish untouched rather than embarrass your hostess in a private home. At a restaurant you may—and should—point out the error to your waiter and ask for a replacement. If the alien object has reached your mouth without your previously noticing it, remove it with your fingers as inconspicuously as possible and place it at the edge of your plate.

Q. . . . *get food stuck in a tooth?*
A. It is not permissible to use a toothpick or to use your fingers to pick at your teeth when at the table. If something stuck in your tooth actually is hurting, excuse yourself from the table and go to the bathroom to remove it. Otherwise, wait until the end of the meal and then go take care of it, asking for a toothpick if necessary.

Q. . . . *spill something?*
A. Pick up jelly, a bit of vegetable, or other solid food with the blade of your knife or a clean spoon. If it has caused a stain, and you are at someone's house, dab a little water from your glass on it with the corner of your napkin. Apologize to your hostess, who, in turn, should not add to your embarrassment by calling attention to the accident.

If you spill wine or water at a formal dinner or in a restaurant, try quietly to attract the attention of the butler or waiter, who will bring a cloth to cover the spot. At an informal dinner without servants, offer to get a cloth or sponge to mop up the liquid and help the hostess clean up in any way you can.

Q. *In whose name are reservations made?*
A. Reservations are usually made in one name only.

They are made in the name of the host or hostess who is giving the dinner party or, if a group of friends plan to meet at a restaurant and each will pay for his own meal, the reservation may be made in the name of the person who is delegated to make it, or in the name of anyone else in the group.

Q. *Why are men's coats and hats checked but women's are not?*
A. Often checkrooms are so small that the attendants will not accept a woman's coat. Other checkrooms will not check a fur coat because the management doesn't want to be responsible for it. Generally, a woman wears her coat until she is seated and then removes it, throwing the shoulders back over her chair. A woman may, of course, check her coat, but if she is wearing a hat she keeps it on.

Q. *Who leads the way to the table, the man or the woman?*
A. Women generally walk behind the headwaiter, and the men follow them. But if a man is giving a dinner for six or more, the women would have to wait at the table until told by their host where to sit. In this case it causes less confusion if he goes in ahead of his guests. When a couple are hosts, the woman seats the guests, usually going first with the most important lady, and the host follows last.

Q. *When a couple is dining at a restaurant with a view who gets the better seat?*
A. The woman is given the better seat, unless for

some reason she prefers another seat. In this case she stands beside the other chair saying, "I'd rather sit here if I may."

Q. *If several people are meeting at a restaurant does the first arriving diner take a table or wait for the others?*
A. The first arrival should wait for the second rather than go in and sit alone, unless the first arrival sees that the restaurant is filling up and there may shortly be no tables left. When two arrive together they should ask to be seated, explaining to the headwaiter that others are joining them and asking him to see that they are directed to the table. This avoids overcrowding the entry and sometimes is the only way of holding a reservation. Some restaurants, however, will not seat a group until all members are present.

Q. *Who gives the order to the waiter? I thought the woman was supposed to tell her choice to the gentleman with whom she was dining and he conveyed it to the waiter. Is this still done?*
A. You are correct in that, for many years, a woman, when dining with a man, never spoke to the waiter herself. This still is correct, but it is equally correct for a woman, particularly when there are more than two people in the party, to give her order directly to the waiter. When the waiter looks straight at a woman and asks, "What kind of dressing would you like on your salad?" it is insulting if she turns away and relays her order through her escort. Many waiters ask the woman for her order first in an effort

to be polite, and there is no reason why she should not answer directly.

Q. *On a restaurant menu what do table d'hôte and à la carte mean?*

A. Table d'hôte means a set price for a complete meal, irrespective of how many courses are offered. "Club" breakfasts and lunches, "blue plate" dinners, or any meals at fixed prices are table d'hôte. Usually, choices of an appetizer or soup, an entrée with vegetables, salad, dessert, and coffee are included in the one price.

Another type of table d'hôte menu is one that has a price beside each entrée. This price varies, with steak, for example, costing more than chicken, but includes the full range of courses at that price. Sometimes a table d'hôte menu will show a price after a particular item, noting, for example, "shrimp cocktail, $3.00 extra." This means the full meal is included in the fixed price, plus the additional amount if shrimp cocktail is ordered instead of an appetizer that does not have its own price.

A la carte means that you order from a list of dishes and you pay the price listed beside each dish—even for your vegetable, salad, and coffee.

Very often a separate card or a box insert on the à la carte menu reads "Special dinner $22.00" or whatever the price may be, so that you can order the special for that price, but that any item taken from the regular bill of fare will be charged for as an extra.

Usually it is easy to know which is which because

a price follows each item on an à la carte menu while the prices are listed only by the entrée or at the top of a table d'hôte menu.

Q. *How do restaurant table manners differ from the manners one uses at home?*

A. Although table manners are much the same whether you are eating at home or at a restaurant, there are a few special problems that do arise when dining out.

> When vegetables and potatoes are served in individual side dishes, you may eat them directly from the small dishes or you may put them on your dinner plate by using a serving spoon or sliding them directly out of the small dish. You may ask the waiter to remove the empty dishes, thus avoiding an overcrowded table.

> You certainly may eat the olives, cherries, or onions served in cocktails, if you wish. If there is no pick, wait until you have drunk enough so you will not wet your fingers and lift out the trimming and eat it with your fingers. Slices of oranges in old-fashioneds are not usually eaten as it is too messy to chew the pulp off the rind.

> When an uncut loaf of bread is placed on the table the host slices or breaks off two or three individual portions and offers them with the rest of the loaf in the breadbasket or on the plate to the people beside him. This is then passed around the table, and each man should

cut or break off a portion for himself and the woman next to him.

If coffee or tea is placed on the table without first having been poured by the waiter, the person nearest the pot should offer to pour, filling his or her own cup last.

If sugar, crackers, cream, or other accompaniments to meals are served with paper wrappers or in plastic or cardboard containers, the wrappers should be crumpled up tightly and either tucked under the rim of your plate or placed on the edge of the saucer or butter plate. Do not put them in the ashtray if there are smokers present, since their lighted cigarettes could easily set the paper on fire.

When jelly or marmalade is served in a plastic or paper container it should be taken out with the butter knife (or dinner knife if there is no butter knife) and put on the bread-and-butter plate. The top is put back in the empty container, which is left on the table beside the butter plate.

Q. *How do you summon the waiter?*
A. In the United States, the usual way is to catch his eye and then raise your hand, first finger pointing up, as if to say "attention" or "listen." If he does not look in your direction you may call "Waiter" (or "Waitress") quietly, or if he is too far away to hear you, ask any other waiter nearby, "Please call our waiter."

"Miss" is also a correct term for a waitress, but "Sir" is not correct for a waiter, whether used by a woman, man, or a youngster.

Q. *After finishing dinner at a restaurant may I freshen my lipstick at the table?*
A. Yes, you may put on lipstick or quickly powder your nose, but to look in a mirror and daub at your face for any length of time is bad manners. Worse yet is to comb or brush your hair at a restaurant table or in any public place. Never rearrange or put your hands to your hair in any place where food is served. This applies to both men and women.

Q. *When dining at a restaurant and discovering friends are also dining there is it permissible to stop by their table for a moment to say hello?*
A. Yes, but just for a moment. If you wish a longer conversation, it is best to arrange to meet later, rather than crowd the restaurant aisle and interrupt your friends' meal, not to mention causing them to stand for any length of time in order to be polite.

All men at a small table rise when a woman is being introduced, as they do whenever a woman stops to talk. When a group is large only those closest to the visitor rise. If a woman stopping at a table is introduced to other women seated there, the latter never rise—even though they be young and the visitor much older.

All the men at the table do not rise when another man stops on his way by. When someone comes up to speak to one of the diners, that man only should rise to shake hands. The visitor should then ask him to please be seated and finish what he has to say.

When a man is seated at a banquette and someone —man or woman—stops by to say "Hello," he merely nods and extends his hand. If he rose either he would get cramps from the crouched position or he would upset the table trying to straighten up, but he may apologize for not rising.

Q. *Most restaurants serve more food than I can eat comfortably at one sitting. May I ask for a doggy bag to bring the food home?*

A. Yes, you may. It is perfectly acceptable if you are comfortable asking and if your portion is just too large for you to finish at the restaurant.

Q. *How do you complain about restaurant service? Do you speak with the server or ask for the manager?*

A. Complaints should be made quietly, without making a fuss or attracting the attention of other diners. They should be made first to the waiter (or the person who commits the error), and if he or she makes no effort to correct the situation, the headwaiter or whoever is in charge of the dining room should be notified. Think twice when your complaint is about laziness or inattention, however, to be sure it is not the waiter's inability to serve too many people. Often the tables are poorly allotted or another waiter is absent and although your waiter is working as hard as he can, he still cannot keep up with the requests of the patrons. It is correct to complain to the manager, but be careful not to put the blame on the waiter who is no happier about the situation than you are. Otherwise, rudeness and laziness should be reported, meat that is not done as you requested should be replaced, and food that is cold should be taken back and reheated.

If, after making a legitimate complaint, you receive no satisfaction from anyone, you may reduce the tip or leave none at all, and avoid that restaurant in the future.

On the other hand, appreciative comments are more than welcome and offered all too infrequently. If your meal and the service were excellent, it is extremely thoughtful to say so.

Q. *How does one host a dinner at a restaurant?*
A. A thoughtful host selects a restaurant he thinks his guest or guests will enjoy and reserves a table. If the host has ordered the dinner ahead of time he or she must try to check the dishes ahead or as they are served to make sure that everything is as requested. If dinner has not been ordered ahead of time, it is the host's duty to take the guest's order and give it to the waiter, or if the party is large, to make sure that the waiter gets the order correctly from each person. In either case, if there are mistakes the host must tactfully and politely see that they are corrected, without embarrassing the guests.

When paying the check, the host does not display the total but puts the money (or the signed credit card form) quietly on the plate and nods to the waiter to remove it. The host indicates to his guests that it is time to leave by rising or with a remark. If the headwaiter has been especially helpful, the host unobtrusively slips a tip (from five dollars depending on the size of the group) into his hand and thanks him as the party is leaving the restaurant.

Q. *Does dining at a smorgasbord, cafeteria-style, or oriental restaurant differ from dining at a restaurant with full table service?*

A. Yes, each is different in several aspects. At a smorgasbord restaurant, individual tables are set as usual, but the meal is not served by waiters. Instead it is set up as a buffet with stacks of small plates at one end to be filled with reasonable amounts of food. Since you are expected to make as many trips as you wish from your seat to the smorgasbord and back, you should never overload your plate and you should only choose foods that go well together each time you serve yourself. Leave your used plate and silver at your table for the waiter to remove while you are helping yourself to your next selection. Start with fish, followed by cold cuts and salad, then by cheeses and a bit of fresh fruit, if you wish. You then choose your hot food, and end with dessert and coffee. It is intended that you take your time to enjoy your dinner. When you are finished, it is expected that you leave your waiter a tip.

A cafeteria is more informal than a smorgasbord. Like a smorgasbord, you serve yourself or are served as you walk through the buffet setup, selecting your complete meal. You pay for your meal at the end of the cafeteria line. Unlike a smorgasbord, if you go back for something else, you again pay for your selection. When the restaurant is crowded and there are no empty tables, it is perfectly all right to take an empty chair at an occupied table, but it is polite to first ask, "Is this seat taken?" or "Do you mind if I sit here?" When there are busboys who carry the trays to the tables, they are generally given a tip of a quarter or fifty cents depending on the cafeteria and the amount of food on the tray. Diners who join strangers at a table are under no obligation to talk to them, but it is polite to respond if he or she speaks to them, and all right to speak first if the other person seems receptive.

Oriental restaurants are like full table service restaurants with the exception in Chinese restaurants that serving dishes are placed in the center of the table so that diners may sample each rather than limit themselves to just one entrée. Some Japanese restaurants request that diners remove their shoes, and some have low tables at which diners sit on cushions on the floor or in a recessed area. If this is uncomfortable or unappealing, most also have regular tables available. Although chopsticks often are set at each place instead of silver, it is perfectly all right to request a knife and a fork.

Getting Along with Others

Q. *What do you consider the hallmarks of being a good neighbor?*

A. Being a good neighbor is mainly a matter of applying the Golden Rule. Treat your neighbors as you would like them to treat you. Allow them their privacy, be tolerant, communicate problems or annoyances directly with them, not with others, and remember that the fact that you live close to each other does not mean you or they should be included in all the other's activities. Even if good neighbors become good friends, you and they have entertainments and activities with other friends and neither you nor they should expect to be included in every one of them.

Q. *How do you deal with ethnic slurs made in a social situation?*

A. You should feel no need to laugh or support such a display of poor taste. You may quietly say, "I don't appreciate that kind of remark," or "I dislike jokes that belittle others." If the offensive slurs continue, you may simply take your leave.

If there are people of the targeted minority group with you or in hearing range, your situation is more embarrassing. Try to change the conversation if you can. If you cannot, avoid the urge to rise to the defense, which might evoke an onslaught even more embarrassing to your friends. Keep your silence, break away as soon as possible, and apologize profusely to them in private.

If you yourself belong to a minority group under attack you have two courses. One, you can ignore it and avoid those people in the future. Or two, you can say, "You must be talking about me. I'm Irish (or whatever it is)." Their shocked embarrassment will be almost as rewarding as their limp efforts to make amends and this may temper their prejudice in the future.

Q. *How do you behave around disabled individuals?*
A. Ideally, you behave just as you would around a person who has no visible handicap. Never stare, and never race in to seize someone's arm or grab a wheelchair. Instead, ask if, and in what way, you can be of assistance. Never make personal remarks or ask personal questions. If the disabled person wishes to discuss his or her condition, he or she may introduce the subject—you may not. If he or she does bring it up, never, never pry into feelings or clinical symptoms—subjects that disabled people may be doing their best to forget.

Q. *I am sometimes embarrassed about not knowing how to act when dealing with hearing impaired or deaf people. Can you offer any hints?*
A. There are many degrees of deafness, from partial

loss of hearing in one ear to complete deafness. If you know that the hearing loss is in one ear, it is considerate to sit on the side of the good ear anywhere it isn't possible to sit face to face. In the case of total hearing loss, the only means of communication is visual, through lipreading.

> When talking, speak slowly and distinctly. Don't use exaggerated lip movements which can be confusing to a person who has been taught to read normal lip movements.

> Don't shout to attract the person's attention. Either it does no good since he can't hear you anyway or it causes distortion since hearing aids are usually adjusted to the normal tone of voice.

> Be patient while talking and willing to repeat or rephrase.

If a relative or close friend is hearing disabled, recommend that he or she wear a hearing aid. There is no more stigma attached to this than there is to wearing glasses. Encourage participation in family and social activities since persons with severe handicaps tend to withdraw into themselves. Try to be sensitive to their reactions, however, because too much pressure can have the opposite effect from that desired. Always include them in conversation, making sure they can see you or the group.

Q. *When I meet blind people I feel I should speak more loudly or otherwise compensate for my being uncomfortable in their presence. How should I act?*

A. What you need to keep in mind is that in every other respect blind people are probably exactly like you. Blind people's other faculties are in no way impaired and actually may be more sensitively developed to compensate for their loss of sight.

When talking, use a normal voice.

Don't avoid the use of the word *see.* A blind person uses it as much as anyone else.

If you are in a room with a blind person it is courteous to describe the room setting and identify the others in the room.

It is correct to ask a blind person if you can help him or her cross the street, but never grasp his or her arm or try to give assistance without first asking whether you may. Let the blind person take your arm rather than you propelling him or her.

When walking with a blind person mention any upcoming obstacles, a step for instance, or a corner to be turned.

If the blind person has a guide dog, do not attempt to play with or distract the dog in any way. Its attention must remain fully on its master, whose safety and well-being may depend entirely on its strict adherence to its training.

Q. *How long should a visitor stay when calling on a sick friend, either at home or in the hospital?*

A. Plan to stay no more than fifteen or twenty minutes, and stick to it, no matter how much your friend may urge you to stay. If other visitors arrive while you are there, leave sooner so that they may have their share of the patient's time without overtiring him or her.

Q. *What can I do if children of friends are brought along on an adults-only visit?*

A. If you wish to be gracious you must invite them in. If the children are small, however, and you have valuable objects which could be damaged, you may ask them to wait a moment while you remove the objects from harm's way, mentioning that you weren't expecting the children.

If you have paper and pencils on hand, you can put them out on your kitchen table for an activity, offer a snack, or find a suitable program on television to keep the children occupied while you and your friends talk.

Other than providing these diversions, you are not obligated to entertain the children and it is the parents' responsibility to be sure they are well behaved and occupied.

Q. *Several of my friends have young children. I do not. What preparations can you suggest be made before they visit?*

A. Remove from low tables breakable articles and things that might be dangerous to a small child. Shut the doors to rooms you wish to make "off limits," and make sure doors to cellar steps and low windows are tightly closed or locked. After completing your safety check, put together a basket of simple toys—coloring books, crayons, blocks, even plastic and wooden cooking utensils and pots and pans. These go a long way toward making the visit enjoyable for both parent and host. If you have absolutely nothing on hand to entertain a child, you may ask that the parents bring a bag of toys so the child or children can be kept busy and happy during the visit. It's also a good idea to have a supply of cookies or crackers and milk or juice on hand to fill in when the novelty of playing in a different environment wears off.

Q. *Am I obligated to entertain an unexpected guest?*
A. No, if you have prior plans, those plans take precedence over entertaining an unexpected guest. If someone arrives unexpectedly from quite a distance and you are planning to leave for a church supper or an informal buffet or cocktail party, check with your host and if all right, suggest your guest go along with you. If, however, you are expected at a small dinner party or for bridge, ask your guest to make him- or herself at home until you return. You should, if possible, find something in the refrigerator or cupboard that will serve as a snack or light meal. You need not make yourself late for your appointment by taking the time to prepare a full meal, although you should show your guest where the ingredients are if he or she wishes to do so.

When the visitor is from nearby, you merely say quite frankly, "I'm terribly sorry, but we were just leaving for the theater. Could you come back another time?" But make the future date right then and there. "Another time" left at that means little, but a firm invitation proves that you would really enjoy a visit at a more convenient time. If your earlier plans were such that they could be carried out on another day, it would of course be more polite to postpone them and stay at home with your visitor.

If you are just about to start your dinner when friends drop in, you must try to make the meal stretch to include them. If they say, "Oh, no thank you—we've just eaten," pull up a chair for them, offer them a cup of coffee or a cold drink, and ask their forgiveness while you finish your meal.

Q. *I've been invited to a friend's country home for the weekend. May I ask to bring my dog along?*
A. No, unless you *know* that they love animals never ask whether you may bring a pet along on a visit. Your host and hostess may be great dog lovers, but they may not want a strange dog who may or may not get along with their dog. You are putting them in a difficult position if they are not enthusiastic about your request. If they make the suggestion, naturally your pet may go. But be sure, before you accept on his behalf, that his behavior will be exemplary. You should never, ever take a dog that is not perfectly house trained, chews things, or will not stay off furniture to anyone else's house.

Telephone Manners

Q. *What is the proper way to answer the telephone?*
A. The best way to answer the telephone at home is still "Hello." There is no need to identify yourself when answering your home telephone.

Q. *Does a caller give his or her name as soon as the phone is answered?*
A. Yes. Not only is it courteous, but it is helpful as well since it gives the person being called the chance to gather papers or whatever may be required by the caller, or to get to a more convenient telephone.

> To a maid or secretary you say: "This is Mrs. Franklin. Is Mrs. Henry in?"
>
> To a child you say: "This is Mrs. Franklin. Is your mother in?"
>
> When you recognize the voice, say: "Hello, John. This is Helen. Is Sue there?"
>
> When the person you are calling answers, say: "Hi, Sue. This is Helen," or "Hello, Mrs. Brooks. This is Helen Franklin."
>
> An older person calling a younger one says: "This is Mrs. Franklin."

A young person calling an older man or woman says: "Hello, Mrs. Knox. This is Janet Frost."

A young child calling a friend says: "Hello, Mrs. Knox. This is Janet Frost. May I please speak to Tammy?"

If a caller does not identify him- or herself, it is correct to ask who is calling, even though it seems a little rude. Actually, the rudeness is on the part of the caller. It is also a matter of safety to inquire as to the identity of the caller. Many calls are made just to find out whether a house is empty, or whether there is a man or an adult at home. If a woman or a child answering doesn't recognize the voice of the caller, he or she must say, "Who is calling, please?" If the name is unfamiliar and the caller does not further identify him- or herself, the answer must not be, "He's not home now." Instead say, "He's busy just now," or "He's not available just now—may he return your call?"

Q. *How do you respond to an invitation made by phone? Must you give an immediate response?*
A. It is incumbent on the person calling to explain the invitation right away: "Hi, Joan, this is Kathleen. We're having a few people in Saturday night for dinner and bridge. Can you and Mark come?" It is most inconsiderate to ask "What are you doing Saturday night?" or "Are you busy Sunday afternoon?" without explaining why you want to know. A "we're not busy" answer could commit one to an evening of opera when one hates opera, and a "we're busy" an-

swer, only to find out the invitation was for something terrific, is disappointing.

Therefore, if the caller does not have the courtesy to explain the invitation but asks only, "Are you busy Saturday night?" you may say, "I don't know if John has made any commitments for Saturday—I'll check with him. Why do you ask?" This forces the caller to issue a proper invitation.

Otherwise, it is very rude to say, "I'll let you know," unless it is immediately followed by an explanation, such as checking with a spouse for previous commitments or "we have tickets for the community theater group that night but perhaps I can exchange them for two on Friday—I'll call you back." Without this definite sort of reason, "I'll let you know" sounds as though you are waiting for a better invitation to come along.

Q. *How do you handle a wrong number?*
A. When you dial a wrong number, don't ask, "What number is this?" Ask instead, "Is this 762-0451?" so that you can look the number up again or dial more carefully the next time.

When you receive a wrong number call, don't give out your number to the caller. Simply inform him or her politely that the wrong number has been dialed.

Q. *How should obscene calls be handled?*
A. Hang up immediately. Don't give the caller the satisfaction of hearing you become upset or even responding. If, as sometimes happens, the call is re-

peated as soon as you hang up, leave the receiver off the hook for a little while.

If you are subjected to such calls regularly, you should of course notify the telephone company. They can try to trace the calls.

There is another effective remedy that will discourage the occasional caller. Keep an ordinary police whistle by the phone and as soon as you hear the first obscene word, blow a hard blast right into the telephone speaker. That caller will drop you from his list of victims there and then.

Q. *Are telephone manners different in a business or social situation?*

A. Yes, business telephone manners differ from at-home telephone manners in several ways. When answering a business call, an assistant or secretary gives his or her employer's name: "Miss Moore's office (or Roz Moore's office). May I help you?" If people answer their phones directly, they usually identify themselves: "Hello, this is Roz Moore," or simply, "Roz Moore."

The caller identifies him- or herself in this case, as with a personal or social call: "Hello. This is Tom Price. Is Miss Moore in?" or "Hello, Miss Moore. This is Tom Price. I'm with the Brownstone Company."

As with an at-home call, it is correct to ask the caller: "May I ask who is calling, please," if he or she fails to identify him- or herself. In an office, a secretary or assistant may also ask, "May I ask what this call is in reference to?" or less bluntly, "Will Miss Moore know what this call is about?"

Although it is not courteous to tie up a telephone line for long at home, it is particularly to be avoided in the office. Long personal conversations are not only out of place, but also wasteful of the time that belongs to the company, not to the employee.

In Houses
of Worship

Q. *How should you dress for a service at a church? A synagogue?*
A. Although clothing restrictions have been greatly relaxed in recent years, the correct dress is still conservative. Even today skirts or conservative pants and jackets for women and suits, slacks, and shirts and/or sport jackets for men are preferable to jeans or shorts for conventional church or synagogue services.

Hats for women are no longer required in any of the Christian churches, but are always correct. In Orthodox Jewish synagogues married women are required to wear some form of head covering.

Men never wear hats in Christian churches—they always do in synagogues. If you are not Jewish and are attending a synagogue for a service, a wedding, or a funeral, there are extra yarmulkes by the entrance. Although it is not your faith or practice, it is expected that you wear a yarmulke or hat when attending a service.

Q. *Do ushers escort everyone to their seats in church?*
A. Not necessarily. Often ushers simply greet worshipers as they enter and let them seat themselves. If

the ushers do seat members of the congregation, they escort them to a pew. A woman does not take the usher's arm unless she needs assistance, but rather follows him as he leads the way to a vacant seat. The usher stands aside while the arrival— whether single or a couple—steps in. Women precede their husbands into the pew, going in far enough to allow room for him—and for children or others who are with them. At a special service, such as a wedding or first communion, early arrivals may keep their aisle seats, standing to let later arrivals get past them. At weekly services, however, those who are already in the pews should move over to make room for later arrivals.

Q. *Is it acceptable to stop and chat or wave to friends before services begin?*
A. It is perfectly correct to nod, smile, or wave at acquaintances before a service starts, and if a friend sits down next to you or in front of you, you may certainly lean over and whisper "Hello." You should not, however, chat, carry on a prolonged conversation, or introduce people to one another until after the service.

Q. *If you decide to attend another church on a regular basis do you owe the clergyman an explanation?*
A. Yes, you owe the clergyman of your former church or synagogue an explanation, both for record-keeping and personal reasons. In some denominations each parish is assessed according to the number of registered members, and therefore its financial condi-

tion can be harmed if a member who leaves is still enrolled but not contributing.

You owe the clergyman a personal explanation of your reasons for leaving, either by letter or in person. Although it may be difficult, try to be very honest and clear. While he may be hurt or upset, your comments may help him to serve the congregation better.

Q. *I occasionally attend church with a friend of another faith. Do I participate in the service?*
A. Unless some part of the service is opposed to your religious convictions, you should attempt to follow the lead of the congregation. Stand when they stand, sing when they sing, pray when they pray. If there is a part in which you do not wish to participate, sit quietly until that portion of the service is over.

A Protestant need not cross himself or genuflect when entering a pew in a Catholic church. Nor must you kneel if your custom is to pray seated—just bend forward and bow your head.

If you are taking communion in a church that is strange to you, watch what the congregation does and follow their lead.

When you attend another church you should make a contribution when the offering plate is passed. This is a way of saying "Thank you" to the church you are visiting.

At Times of Loss & Grieving

Q. *When and how are calls of condolence made?*
A. They should be made as soon as possible after hearing of the death. If the friends are very close, you will probably be admitted to speak to them. If you are, you should offer your services to help in any way you can. There are countless ways to be helpful, from assisting with such needs as food and child care, to sending telegrams, making phone calls, and answering the door. If they do not need anything, you offer your sympathy and leave without delay.

A condolence call to a Jewish family is made during the seven days following the burial. This period of mourning is known as sitting *shivah* (*shivah* is the Hebrew word for seven). The call is made to the home of those in mourning and gives you an opportunity to express your sympathy to the bereaved.

When you are not well acquainted with the family and do not wish to intrude on their privacy, you may leave your card with "with deepest sympathy" written across the top.

At a funeral home you sign the register and offer the family your sympathy in person. If you do not see them, you should write a letter of sympathy at once. Telephoning is not improper, but it may cause inconvenience by tying up the line, which is always needed at these times for notifying members of the family and for making necessary arrangements.

Visits of condolence need not be returned.

Q. *How should relatives be notified of a death?*
A. Members of the family and other close friends should be called on the telephone. Other relatives, even those who live at some distance, should also be called, but if expense is a factor, friends and other more distant relatives may be notified by telegram.

Q. *If the family elects to have a newspaper notice of death how is it worded?*
A. Newspaper notices usually contain the date of death, names of the immediate family, hours and locations where friends may call on the family, place and time of the funeral, and frequently, a request that a contribution be given to a charity instead of flowers being sent to the deceased.

The word *suddenly* is sometimes inserted immediately after the deceased's name to indicate that there had not been a long illness, or that the death was by accident. Often "After a long illness" is inserted to communicate that information.

Instead of "Friends may call at (address)" the phrase "Reposing at Memorial Funeral Home" is commonly used.

The deceased's age is not generally included unless he or she is very young or the age is needed to establish further identification.

Daughters of the deceased are listed before sons. A woman's notice always includes her given and maiden name for purposes of identification. The same is true when married daughters and sisters are mentioned.

The use of adjectives such as *beloved, loving, devoted,* etc., is optional.

A woman's notice might read:

Cohen—Helen Weinberg, on May 13. [Beloved] wife of Isaac, [loving] mother of Rebecca, Paul, and Samuel, [devoted] sister of Anna Weinberg Gold and Paul Weinberg. Services Thursday, May 14, 2:00 P.M., at Star Funeral Home, 41 Chestnut Street, Pittsburgh. In lieu of flowers, contributions may be sent to the United Jewish Appeal, or your favorite charity.

A man's notice might read:

Johnson—Michael B., on December 12, 1988. [Beloved] husband of the late Kathleen Stuart Johnson. [Devoted] father of Erin Johnson Flynn, Brad S., and Sean R. Friends may call at 44 Wendt Avenue, Harrison, New York, on Friday, December 15, 2–5. Funeral service Saturday, December 16, 11:30 A.M., St. John's Lutheran Church, Mamaroneck, New York.

An obituary may also be run. The family may submit it, but it is the option of the editors to decide whether they wish to print it or not. In the event that one is submitted, it includes the residence of family members listed (Brad S. of New York City, Sean R. of Mamaroneck) and information about the previous activities, memberships, affiliations, and career of the deceased. If the person who died was prominent in the community, it is probable that the newspapers have a file on him or her. The information they have should be checked by someone who is acquainted with the facts so that no errors will be made in the published obituary.

Q. *What does "in lieu of flowers" mean?*
A. It means that the family requests a contribution to a specific charity instead of flowers and believes the contribution will help them to feel that some good has come from their loss. A check is sent to the charity with a note saying "This donation is sent in memory of Mrs. Roy Haskell of 10 Stetson Way, Austin, Texas." Your address should appear on the note.

Occasionally a notice reads, "Please send a contribution to your favorite charity." You are free to choose whichever one you wish, but it is thoughtful to select one that might also mean something to the bereaved family.

The amount of the contribution is up to you. However, you should not give less than you would have paid for a flower arrangement.

If no "in lieu of" appears in the notice, you should send flowers.

Another option is to send a plant or flower arrangement to the family a few days after the funeral as an indication of your continuing sympathy and love. Sometimes friends do this instead of funeral flowers or contributions; others do it in addition to one or the other. Cards accompanying these flowers or plants should not mention the recent loss, but may simply say, "With love from us all" or "With love."

Q. *What role can friends play immediately following a death?*
A. In addition to helping with family meals, child care, sending telegrams, making telephone calls, and answering the door, they can help organize food if there is to be a gathering of family and friends after the funeral. They can offer to stay at the house during the funeral service (often houses are robbed during a funeral when it is known that no one will be at home) or they can offer to be in charge of flowers, collecting all the accompanying cards one hour before the service and writing a description of the flowers so a later note, from the family, can properly thank the giver, including a specific mention of the "beautiful coral roses" or the "laurel wreath with gardenias." Often this service is performed by the funeral home. If it is not, it is a tremendous help to the family to have someone take care of it for them.

Other services friends can provide include offering to have out-of-town relatives attending the funeral stay at their homes and offering to drive family members to and from the funeral home or the church or synagogue or to run other errands.

Q. *Who generally serve as pallbearers? May someone refuse to serve as a pallbearer? What are honorary pallbearers and what role do they play in a funeral?*

A. Generally, close friends of the deceased serve as pallbearers. They may be asked when they come to pay their respects, or by telephone or telegram. Members of the immediate family are never chosen, as their place is with the women of the family.

One cannot refuse an invitation to be a pallbearer except for illness or absence from the city.

Honorary pallbearers serve only at church funerals. They do not carry the coffin. This service is performed by the assistants of the funeral director, who are expertly trained. The honorary pallbearers sit in the first pews on the left, and after the service leave the church two by two, walking immediately in front of the coffin.

Q. *If you extend an expression of sympathy at a funeral home do you also write a condolence note?*

A. A visitor who sees and personally extends his sympathy at the funeral home need not write a note of condolence, unless he wishes to write an absent member of the family. Those who merely sign the register and do not speak with family members should, in addition, write a note.

Q. *Who may stop by a funeral home to pay his respects? Who attends a funeral?*

A. Anyone who wishes to express his sympathy to the family of the deceased may stop by a funeral home and pay his respects. People who do not feel they are close enough to intrude on the privacy of the bereaved may stop in at times other than those during which the family is there and sign the register.

If the newspaper notice reads "Funeral private," only those who have received an invitation from the family may go. If the hour and the location of the service are printed in the paper, that is considered an invitation to anyone who wishes to attend. All members of the family should find out when the funeral is to take place and go to it without waiting to be notified.

A divorced man or woman should go to the funeral of the deceased if the latter had not remarried and there are children involved. Even if the deceased had remarried, the former spouse should attend if cordial relations have been maintained with the family of the deceased, although he or she should sit in the rear and not attempt to join the family. If the deceased had remarried, and there was ill feeling, the former spouse should not attend, but should send flowers and a brief note of condolence.

Q. *Does everyone wear black when attending a funeral?*

A. No, it is no longer considered necessary to wear black unless you sit with the family or have been asked to be one of the honorary pallbearers. However, you should wear clothes that are subdued in color and inconspicuous. On no account should children be put into black at any time. They wear their best conservative clothes to a funeral.

Q. *Does everyone who attends a funeral also attend the burial?*
A. Only if the burial is in the churchyard or within walking distance of the church does the congregation follow the family to the graveside. Otherwise, those attending the funeral, wherever the services are held, do not go to the interment unless they are family members or close friends.

Q. *What is a memorial service? How does it differ from a funeral? Does a memorial service replace a funeral service?*
A. A memorial service takes the place of a funeral, after the deceased has been buried or cremated privately or when the deceased has died in another country or perhaps in an airplane accident or accident at sea. If it takes place very shortly after the death, the service is very much like a funeral service. If it takes place much later, however, it is more often very brief. In general outline: Two verses of a hymn are sung, short prayers follow, and a very brief address is given about the work and life of the one for whom the service is held. It is closed with a prayer and a verse or two of another hymn.

Usually no flowers are sent except those for the altar.

An alternative to a memorial service is a "Service of Thanksgiving for the Life of (John Doe)." The service is simple, consisting of two or three tributes or eulogies given by friends or relatives, a prayer by the clergyperson, and perhaps two or three hymns or musical offerings that were favorites of the deceased.

Q. *How does a family acknowledge expressions of sympathy?*
A. Flowers, messages, Mass cards, personal condolences, contributions, and special kindnesses must all be acknowledged. Printed condolence cards with no personal message added and calls at the funeral home need not be acknowledged.

A personal message on a fold-over card is the preferable form for acknowledging expressions of sympathy. The note may be brief, but should be warm and mention the specific kindness or floral arrangement, etc. Printed or engraved cards may also be used, as long as a personal handwritten note is added below the printed message. If the condolences have come from strangers, however, as is often the case when a public figure or a member of his family dies and hundreds of impersonal messages are received, an engraved or printed card need not include a handwritten addition. Printed cards usually read:

The family of
Harrison L. Winthrop
wish to thank you for
your kind expression of sympathy

If the list of personal acknowledgments to be sent is very long, or if the person who has received the flowers and messages is really unable to perform the task of writing, a member of the family or a near friend may write for him or her: "Mother asks me to thank you for your beautiful flowers and kind message of sympathy."

Letters must also be written to honorary pallbearers and ushers, thanking them for their service and perhaps noting how much their presence meant to the family.

Q. *Who should attend a funeral of a business associate?*
A. If the funeral is not private, anyone who worked closely with the deceased should attend the funeral, even though he or she may not know any of the family members.

Q. *Who serves as ushers at a funeral or memorial service and what do they do?*
A. Ushers may be chosen in addition to, or in place of, pallbearers. Although funeral directors will supply men to perform the task, it is infinitely better to select men from the family (not immediate family) or close friends, who will recognize those who come and seat them according to their closeness to the family or according to their own wishes.

At both a funeral and a memorial service, ushers hand those who enter a bulletin of the service, if one is used, and show them to a pew. They do not offer their arms to a woman unless she needs assistance, but walk slightly ahead. At a memorial service, they also ask people to sign a register, if the family wishes, before entering.

When there are no pallbearers the ushers sit in the front pews on the left and exit ahead of the coffin as pallbearers would. If there are pallbearers the ushers remain at the back of the church.

Communications

Q. *I am often at a loss about starting a conversation with a stranger. Can you give me any hints to get the conversation going?*

A. In talking to a person you have just met and about whom you know nothing, the best approach is to try one topic after another, usually not by asking questions that can be answered "yes" or "no" but by asking his advice or opinion. From his answer, hopefully you can carry on a conversation. Don't be afraid of a period of silence and chatter about anything at all just to fill it. Think before you speak. Dorothy Sarnoff wrote: "*I* is the smallest letter in the alphabet. Don't make it the largest word in your vocabulary. Say, with Socrates, not 'I think,' but 'what do you think?'" You will leave the person with the impression that you are an interesting and interested person and, just as important, a good listener when you don't monopolize the conversation out of panic that nothing will be said if you don't carry the conversational ball all by yourself. Of course, take your turn, describing something you have been doing or an interesting article you have read, but then stop and ask your new acquaintance his opinion about or experiences with the topic.

Q. *How do you handle a tactless person who makes his prejudices known in social situations?*
A. If you find another's opinion totally unacceptable, try to change the subject as soon as possible. If that doesn't work, excuse yourself from the conversation, particularly if you care intensely about the subject and might become emotional in your response.

Q. *How do you answer personal questions about your age or the cost of a gift?*
A. If you are asked your age and would prefer not to give it, you might say, "Old enough to know better," or you can be as indefinite as, "Over twenty-one," or you can use my particular favorite, "Thirty-nine (or forty-nine, or whatever) and holding."

When you are asked the cost of a gift or your house or a piece of clothing, you are under no obligation to answer with the price. You can simply say, "I don't know (or remember) what it cost," or you can say, "I'd rather not talk about that, if you don't mind. With the cost of living what it is, the whole subject is too depressing . . ." and change the subject.

Q. *My penmanship isn't very good. May I type my personal letters?*
A. Yes, it is absolutely correct to type a personal letter, although a thank-you note, letter of condolence, and an invitation via an informal note should be

handwritten, unless it is impossible because of arthritis, for example, for one to hold a pen.

Q. *Under what circumstances are thank-you notes obligatory, optional, or unnecessary?*
A. The most important qualifications of a thank-you letter are that it sound sincere and that it be written promptly. You use the expressions most natural to you and write as enthusiastically as you would speak. The chart on pages 82–85 tells you when thank-you notes are obligatory, optional, or unnecessary.

Q. *What should I do when I don't receive any acknowledgment for a gift?*
A. If you delivered the gift in person, you know it was received and that the recipient is exercising bad manners. If, however, you mailed the gift or had it sent from a store and have received no acknowledgment after three months at the outside, you must write and ask whether or not it was received.

It is inexcusable not to thank the donor for any gift so if your letter embarrasses the recipient, that is fine. She or he should be embarrassed and perhaps will remember better manners in the future.

One suggestion is to send all gifts insured. You then have a good reason to write and say, "Since I haven't heard from you I assume the gift I sent was lost. If that is so I would like to put a claim in for the insurance, so would you let me know as soon as possible whether you received it or not."

When the gift in question is a check, you might write, "I am quite concerned about the check I sent

Thank-You Notes

Occasion	Obligatory
Dinner parties	Only if you are a guest of honor.
Overnight visits	Always except in the case of close friends or relatives whom you see frequently. Then, a telephone call would serve the purpose.
For birthday, anniversary, Christmas, and other gifts	Always, when you have not thanked the donor in person. Here again, a phone call to a very close friend or relative is sufficient.
Shower gifts	If the donor was not at the shower or you did not extend verbal thanks.
Gifts to a sick person	Notes to out-of-towners and calls or notes to close friends are obligatory as soon as the patient feels well enough.
For notes of condolence	Thank-yous should be sent for all notes of condolence except for printed cards with no personal message.
For congratulatory cards or gifts	All personal messages must be acknowledged.

Optional or Unnecessary

Otherwise, always appreciated but not necessary if you have thanked your hostess when leaving.

It is never wrong to send a note in addition to your verbal thanks.

Many women like to add a written note to their verbal thanks, but it is not necessary.

Form letters from firms need not be acknowledged.

continued

Occasion	Obligatory
Wedding gifts	*Obligatory*—even though verbal thanks have been given. All wedding gifts must be acknowledged within three months, but preferably as the gifts arrive.
When a hostess receives a gift after visitors have left	Even though the gift is a thank-you itself, the hostess must thank her visitors, especially if the gift has arrived by mail, so that the visitor will know it has been received.
When a client is entertained by a sales representative	

you for your birthday. It has been cashed and returned to me, but since I have received no word from you I am worried that it fell into the wrong hands and it was not you who cashed it. Would you let me know?''

Q. *What are visiting cards and how are they still used today?*

A. Visiting cards, or calling cards, are small (usually 3 to 3½ inches wide and from 2¼ to 2½ inches high) engraved cards made of white or cream-white glazed or unglazed bristol board of medium thickness. They are engraved only with the name of the person who

Optional or Unnecessary

Even though the entertainment is charged to the sales representative's company it would not be remiss to send a note. It is not necessary, but might help to ensure a good relationship.

will use them or, in some cases, with the names of a couple. A joint card is often referred to as a "husband-and-wife" card or a "Mr. and Mrs." card.

Visiting cards once were used in great quantities when people called at the houses of friends and acquaintances. This rarely is done anymore, except in military and diplomatic circles. Today visiting cards are used primarily as enclosures with gifts and flowers, and as invitations that are delivered by hand. (They are too small to send through the mail.) A personal note or the specifics of the invitation are generally added by hand at the top of the card. When visiting

Mrs. William Goadby Post

Mr. William Goadby Post

Mr. and Mrs. William Goadby Post

cards are used for theses purposes, it is necessary to order a supply of matching envelopes.

Very often, informals are ordered instead of visiting cards. They are more practical since they may be used for thank-you notes and other correspondence as well.

Husband-and-wife cards may not be used by a woman alone or a man alone, only when they are visiting or sending a gift as a couple.

Q. *Besides one's parents who should be told about a living-together relationship?*
A. Relatives need be informed of your new situation in life only as they are involved with your life: siblings whom you see or correspond with—yes; aunts, uncles, and cousins with whom you are in close contact—yes; but the "funeral and wedding relations"—no need.

Of course you tell the friends you see frequently and those to whom you write often. In short, tell anybody who will meet your partner on more than a casual basis and anyone with whom you regularly share the news of your life. You need not announce your relationship to business associates unless you see them socially, but if it comes up in conversation, do not hide it.

In addition to friends and family, it is a good idea to tell the letter carrier that Alan Burnett or Marianne Welch will also be receiving mail in your box from now on. There is no need for further explanation.

Tell your landlord, the superintendent, and the doorman if you have them, so that they will treat your new roommate as another tenant, not as a visitor.

Unless you know your neighbors well there is no need to say anything to them, other than a casual introduction if you meet. Nor is there any need to alert local shops. When your partner orders purchases to be delivered, the address given will be adequate.

Q. *What do you call your living-together partner?*
A. I have come to the conclusion that the best form of introduction is to use no word of definition at all. Merely say, "This is Belinda Geddes," or "I'd like you to meet Charles Morley." It is simply not necessary in an introduction to indicate the relationship between two people when you are at a gathering where relationships make little difference. In a small group where who relates to whom has more importance, all you need add to the introduction is "the man (or woman) I live with."

Q. *Whom do you tell about a divorce?*

A. Tell those to whom it makes a difference. Tell your parents and close family and good friends. Tell your business associates only if they are good friends. Tell the landlord or superintendent and doorman if one of you is keeping the apartment. At times it is necessary to tell doctors and dentists if your children's bills are to be sent to the parent not in custody of the children, and it is wise to notify the school office and your children's teachers, since it is important that they know of any situation that may have impact on your children's behavior and school performance. Otherwise it is not necessary to tell anyone. The situation will become public knowledge very quickly as soon as one member of the couple moves out. The one who moves may have change-of-name and -address cards printed, and of course his or her Christmas cards will serve as announcements. A note may be added to them—"As you can see, Bob and I are divorced. Hope to hear from you at my new address."

Under no circumstances should printed divorce announcements be sent out. It is in the worst of taste.

Gifts & Giving

Q. *When is it acceptable to give money as a gift?*
A. In most cases a gift other than money is the proper choice, but there are some exceptions. Many ethnic groups traditionally give money as a wedding gift, and often money is given for a religious confirmation, a first communion, a bar or bas mitzvah, and a graduation. Another occasion for which a gift of money is not inappropriate is a fiftieth anniversary. Many older couples, perhaps living on a small pension or social security, appreciate cash more than gifts, which they neither need nor have room for.

For people who dislike the idea of giving a check or cash, a gift certificate is a good compromise.

Q. *Should gifts be opened at a party?*
A. Yes. Half the fun of giving and receiving presents at any party is to see and enjoy what everyone else brought. The nicest way to do this is to have all the presents collected in one place until everyone has arrived, at which time the guest of honor opens them. The recipient reads the cards enclosed and shows enthusiasm for each gift, no matter how peculiar some

may be. If anyone has given money instead of a present, the amount should not be mentioned but the recipient may well say something like, "This is a really welcome contribution toward the china we are saving for," or whatever else may be appropriate.

On occasions when gifts are not necessarily expected, but two or three people bring them regardless, they are opened in the donor's presence but without drawing the attention of the other guests. This might happen, for instance, when a couple brings a gift to a dinner hostess. She must show her appreciation, but making a display of the present could embarrass guests who did not bring one.

Q. *How can you respond when someone arrives with an unexpected gift at Christmastime?*
A. Unless you have a supply of small gifts or tins of home-baked goods ready for such an emergency you can only say, "Thanks so much—but you shouldn't have done this," to indicate that you do not expect to start an annual exchange of gifts.

Q. *A close friend with whom I usually exchange gifts will be celebrating a birthday soon. The birthday party invitation reads, "no gifts, please." I'm confused— should I bring a gift or not?*
A. No, you should not take a gift to the party since the invitation specifically states not to, but you may drop your gift off or have it delivered to her at her home before or after the party.

Q. *What gifts are returned when an engagement is broken? What about wedding gifts if the marriage lasts only a short time?*

A. All gifts except those that are monogrammed should be returned if an engagement is broken, including the engagement ring and any gifts of value received from a fiancé or fiancée. Shower gifts, too, should be returned if the marriage is called off. Once the wedding has taken place, however, gifts are not returned, no matter how short-lived the marriage, unless the wedding is annulled before the couple lives together.

Q. *What do I do if a gift arrives broken?*

A. If it arrives directly from a local store, take it with its wrappings to the shop where it was purchased. If it comes from another city or a mail-order company, return it by mail, accompanied by a letter explaining how it arrived. Any good store or company will replace the merchandise on reasonable evidence that it was received in a damaged condition. Do not involve the donor in this or even let him or her know what happened if you can possibly avoid doing so.

If the package was packed and mailed by the donor, not a store, and it was insured, you must let the sender know so he or she can collect the insurance and replace the gift. If the package was not insured, it is best not to mention the damaged condition since the sender will feel obligated to replace the gift at his own, duplicate expense.

Q. *May duplicate wedding gifts be exchanged? Do I tell the donor?*

A. Yes, duplicate wedding gifts may be exchanged, so long as they are not from the bridegroom's family. Only if told by them to exchange the gift for something else may the bride do so.

When a duplicate gift is received from someone who lives far away and is not likely to visit the bride and groom soon, the couple need not mention the fact that they are exchanging a present on their thank-you note. However, it would be wise to explain the exchange to someone who will be in their house and will surely notice the absence of the gift. If you do mention the exchange to the donor, it is important to mention in your thank-you note that you are enjoying what you got as a replacement, thanks to them.

Q. *How soon after receiving a gift should the thank-yous be written?*

A. Thank-yous should be written promptly, particularly when a gift is received through the mail or United Parcel Service and the donor has no way of knowing if you received it or not. Although it is preferable that the bride and groom acknowledge all gifts as they are received, they may, if necessary, take up to three months, at the outside, to send their thank-yous.

Tipping

Q. *What guidelines can you give for tipping?*
A. I believe firmly that a tip should be merited. Where service is bad and the personnel deliberately rude, inattentive, or careless, the amount should be reduced. If it is bad enough, no tip should be left at all, and you should bring the situation to the attention of the manager. On the other hand, rewarding good service more generously is just as important since service people depend on tips to augment their usually low salary. Their effort to provide excellent service therefore should be appreciated.

With this as a basic guideline, the chart on the following pages gives general standards for tipping in most parts of the United States.

When Dining

Recipient	Amount or Percentage to Tip
Bartender	15 percent of the bar bill if you have drinks at the bar before going to your table. It is given to him when he gives you your check or, if the bar bill is added to your dinner check, before you leave the bar.
Busboys	No tip except in cafeterias when busboy carries your tray to the table, in which case tip 25 or 50 cents.
Caterers	
at clubs or restaurants	If the service charge is added to the bill (usually 15 percent) the host is not obligated to do more unless he wishes to do so, except to the person in charge—headwaiter, maître d', or whoever it may be—who receives a separate tip of $5 to $10 or more, depending on the size and elaborateness of the party. If no service charge is added, the host gives the person in charge 15 percent of the bill and asks that he divide it among the waiters, plus $10 or more for the person in charge.

When Dining *(cont.)*

Recipient	Amount or Percentage to Tip
at home	Approximately 20 percent of the bill is given to be divided among the bartender, waiters and waitresses by the host before they leave, if gratuities are not to be included in the bill.
Checkroom attendant	Even if there is a charge for checking your coat, tip the attendant. When the charge is 75 cents per coat, tip 25 cents. If no charge, tip 50 cents per coat for more than one coat but $1 for one coat. No extra tip for parcels unless there are many.
Headwaiters	At a restaurant you patronize regularly, $5 to $10 from time to time.
	When he has done nothing but seat you and hand you a menu, no matter how many in your party, no tip.
	$5 or more if he arranges a special table, cooks a special dish in front of you, or offers other special services.
	Hand him your tip as you leave the restaurant.

When Dining *(cont.)*

Recipient	Amount or Percentage to Tip
Musicians	No tip to strolling player unless he plays specific request. Then the usual tip is $1. If several members of a large party make requests, up to $5.
	$1 to $2 to pianist or organist for playing your request.
Waiters and waitresses	15 percent of the bill, slightly higher for extraordinarily good service. 20 percent in very elegant restaurants.
	If hosting dinner party of ten, twelve, or more, 15 percent of bill is divided among the waiters and waitresses who serve you.
	Never less than 15 cents for cup of coffee or soft drink only. Never less than 25 cents at lunch counter.
	In restaurant, tip left on tray on which check is brought or added to credit card.
	At lunch counter, tip left on counter.

When Dining *(cont.)*

Recipient	Amount or Percentage to Tip
Washroom attendants	Never less than 50 cents, sometimes $1 in expensive restaurant. Tip placed in dish or plate for that purpose. If attendant does nothing but sit and look at you, no tip necessary.
Wine steward	15 percent of wine bill when you are getting ready to leave. If wine charged to credit card separate from dinner order, tip may be added to charge slip at the time bill is presented.

While Traveling

Recipient	Amount or Percentage to Tip
Airplanes	Skycaps (porters) receive 50 cents a bag or $2 or more for a baggage cart full of luggage. (No tips ever for stewardesses, stewards, hostesses, or flight officers.)
Bus tours; charter buses	$5 to $10 on a long tour to both driver and guide, depending on length of tour, unless gratuities are included in the fare.
	No tip to charter and sightseeing bus drivers. Optional 50 cents to $1 to guides or driver-guides.
Cruise ships	
cabin and dining stewards	Check with travel agent. Often $1 to $1.50 per day depending on which "class" you travel and the services you receive.
	or
	10 to 15 percent of total fare, one half of which is divided between cabin steward and dining room steward. The other half divided between head dining steward and deck steward.
	Tip an appropriate proportion at end of each week so personnel has cash to spend during stops in ports.

While Traveling *(cont.)*

Recipient	Amount or Percentage to Tip
lounge and bar stewards	15 percent of bill at time of service, never less than a quarter.
wine steward	15 percent of total wine bill.
bath steward	If no private bath, $1 when you reserve time for your bath.
cabin boys	At least 25 cents for each errand performed.
porter	$2 to $5 for heavy trunks, $1 per bag for suitcases.
cruise director	No tip ever.
ship's officers	No tip ever.
when gratuities included in fare	$1 to $2 to someone who has been especially helpful.
Hotels and full-service motels (stays of one week or less)	
bellman	$1 per bag—more if very heavy—plus 50 cents for opening room, in large cities.
	50 cents per bag plus 50 cents to $1 for opening room in smaller cities.

While Traveling *(cont.)*

Recipient	Amount or Percentage to Tip
chambermaid	$5 to $10 a week per person in first-class hotel.
	$3 to $5 a week in small, inexpensive hotel.
	No tip if staying only one night.
	Give tip in person if possible. If not, leave on bureau in envelope marked "chambermaid," or give to desk clerk and ask that he or she deliver it.
desk clerk	No tip unless special service is rendered, in which case $10 is ample.
dining room waiter	In first-class hotel restaurant, 15 percent of the bill.
doorman	50 cents per bag if he takes luggage into the hotel.
	No tip if he puts bag on sidewalk.
	25 cents for calling a taxi or, if you are staying longer than a day or two, $1 or $2 at end of each week.
garage valet parking service	$1 in large cities and 50 cents in smaller cities each time car is delivered.

While Traveling *(cont.)*

Recipient	Amount or Percentage to Tip
headwaiter	When you leave, tip in proportion to the services rendered: $2 to $3 a week if he has done little, $10 a week if he has been especially attentive.
	No tip needed for one-night stay.
room waiter	15 percent of bill for each meal. This is in addition to hotel fee for room service.
valet	No tip.
Taxis	25 cents minimum for fare up to $1.50. For higher fares, tip 15 percent of meter.
	Same for unmetered cabs; pay 15 percent of fare.
Trains	
bar or club car waiters	15 percent of bill, as well as 25 to 50 cents for delivering setups to your sleeping car.
dining car waiters	15 percent of the bill and never less than 25 cents.
luggage porters	50 cents to $1 in addition to fixed rate fee.
sleeping car porter	At least $2 per person per night—more if he has given additional service other than making up berths.

At Health or Sport Clubs

Recipient	Amount or Percentage to Tip
Golf caddies	15 percent of the regular club charge for eighteen holes, closer to 20 percent for nine holes.
Instructors	No tip.
Locker-room attendant	50 cents at time service rendered if he or she provides towels or other personal attention.
Masseur	20 percent of the cost of the massage.
Other personnel	Generally no tip at time of service. Often a members' collection at Christmastime for employees' fund.
	Give additional tips, usually $5 to $10, depending on type of club and amount of service, to any employee who gives you personal attention—washroom attendant, locker-room attendants, headwaiter, etc.
	Sometimes additional tips for special services throughout year.
	Guests do not tip unless residents for a time, in which case, if no service charge added to bill, tip as you would in a first-class hotel.

Personal & Professional Services

Recipient	Amount or Percentage to Tip
Answering service	Minimum of $5 per operator who has a shift on your service, at Christmastime.
Au pair or live-in child care/house-keeper	One week's extra salary at Christmastime, plus small gifts from children
Baby-sitters	For steady baby-sitters, double an average night's salary at Christmas —or a small gift from the children is thoughtful—in addition to tip at time of service, usually the equivalent of approximately one half to one hour's pay.
Barber	
for a child	In a rural area, 25 to 50 cents. In a city, 50 cents to $1 is about average.
for an adult	Since the cost is higher than for a child, the tip should be correspondingly higher. $1 to $2 to the manicurist and for a shampoo, shave, etc., an equivalent amount depending on the type of shop and the number of services used. A regular customer does not tip the shop owner for each haircut, but gives him or her a gift at Christmas.

Personal & Professional Services *(cont.)*

Recipient	Amount or Percentage to Tip
Beauty salon	15 percent to one stylist who shampoos, cuts, and sets or drys. 20 percent if several stylists divide services, as follows: 10 percent to the person who cuts, 10 percent divided among the others. Generally no tip to a proprietor who cuts or sets your hair, although 10 percent is acceptable if you wish. If it is your first visit, watch what other customers do or ask the receptionist. Regular customers give a small gift at Christmas to the proprietor, stylist, and shampooer.
Butcher	If you receive regular deliveries one or more times a week, tip at least $5 per service deliverer at Christmastime.
Cleaner	If your dry cleaning is picked up and delivered regularly one or more times a week, tip at least $5 per service deliverer at Christmas.
Commercial messengers	If you use services on regular basis, $5 to $10 at Christmastime.
Dairy	If the dairy delivers regularly, once or more times a week, tip at least $5 per service deliverer at Christmastime.

Personal & Professional Services *(cont.)*

Recipient	Amount or Percentage to Tip
Diaper service	$5 at Christmastime or, if you keep the service for less than one year, when you terminate the service.
Florists	50 cents to $1 to delivery person when you order flowers or floral arrangements sent to your home or when flowers are sent to you by someone else.
Garbage collectors	$5 to $10 per crew member at Christmastime for private service workers. Same to municipal workers if not in violation of local law.
Grocery loaders	50 cents for normal number of bags placed in car. $1 for large week's marketing.
Hospital staff	No money tips. It is proper to bring candy or the like that can be shared by all the staff caring for the patient. Give three of whatever the gift is, marked "1st shift," "2nd shift," "3rd shift." Otherwise the shift on duty at the time will enjoy it but seldom leave any for the other shifts that have cared for the patient too.
private duty nurses	For prolonged duty, Christmas gift or gift on departing, but no money.

Personal & Professional Services *(cont.)*

Recipient	Amount or Percentage to Tip
Hotels, residential	Permanent or long-term residents tip on monthly or even twice-yearly basis according to quality of service.
Household helpers	
live-in help	$5 to $10 when extra work is required for large party.
	One week's pay at Christmastime.
part-time housecleaners	Approximately one week's pay at Christmastime.
when a guest in a private home	After weekend visit, $3 to host's maid and/or cook for a single guest, $5 for a couple.
	No tip ever to servants at a dinner party.
Laundry service	If regular pick-up and delivery, at least $5 at Christmastime.
Letter carriers	According to the United States Postal Service, it is illegal to tip your letter carrier.
Movers and furniture deliverers	No tip for one or two crates or pieces of furniture. For larger loads or if movers perform special services (put furniture in place, lay carpets, etc.) at least $5 per person.

Personal & Professional Services *(cont.)*

Recipient	Amount or Percentage to Tip
Newspaper carriers	$5 to $15 at Christmas, depending on number of days carrier delivers and the quality of service. 25 to 50 cents per week paid at time of regular collection.
Parking attendants	50 cents to attendant who delivers car from garage in small cities; $1 in large cities.
	When you rent garage space monthly, attendants are not tipped for delivery but are given tips at Christmastime and occasionally throughout year for special services, usually $5 each time.
Residential building employees at Christmas	Depending on size of building and staff and amount of services:
superintendent	$30 to $40 if he lives in, less if a janitor or other staff member does repairs.
doormen	$10 to $30 to each doorman, plus occasional tips of $1 to $5 for special services, hailing taxicabs, accepting deliveries, etc.
janitor	Janitor or regular handyman, $10 to $20 depending on amount of service rendered.

Personal & Professional Services *(cont.)*

Recipient	Amount or Percentage to Tip
elevator operators	$10 to $15.
Shoeshines	50 cents for shoes, $1 for boots at time service rendered.
Ushers	No tip at movie theater, concert hall, opera house, or theater.
	50 cents to $1 per party at an arena, for boxes and loges. No tip necessary in upper balconies and bleachers.

Q. *I'm vacationing in Europe this year. Is tipping there done the same way as here at home?*
A. No, generally it is a different system. In most European restaurants and hotels, a 15 percent (approximate) service charge is added to your bill. You are not expected to give additional tips. Do not tip the bellboy, maid, or concierge. Do not tip the waiters beyond service charge and if you wish, any small coins returned to you as change.

When no service charge is added to your bill, or if you think it is too low, tip exactly as you would in the United States.

Theater ushers are tipped in Europe, usually the equivalent of a quarter, but not in England. In England, there is generally a charge for the program instead.

Names & Titles
on the Job

Q. *When starting a new job how do I know if I should use first names, or address people by title and last name?*
A. At the beginning, it is safest to use "Mr.," "Mrs.," "Miss," or "Ms." If they say, "Please call me Mary (or Jim)," then you may feel free to do so. In return you should suggest that they call you by your first name as well.

Q. *Occasionally some of my company's clients call me "dear." Often the comment comes from older clients, and perhaps they don't realize they are offending anyone, so I am hesitant to say anything. How can I politely encourage these clients to call me by my given name?*
A. It is appropriate for you to say, "My name is Mary, not 'dear,' and I really prefer to be called Mary, please." Be sure, however, that you say it kindly and with the best of manners since, as you note, it is usually not intended as an offense.

Q. *Does the salutation for a business letter differ from that on a personal letter?*
A. If you don't know the person to whom you are writing, use "Dear Sir," "Dear Madam," or "Dear Sir

or Madam." If you do know him personally, your salutation uses the name you ordinarily call the person. If, when you speak to the vice-president of marketing, you call him "Jim," you would begin your letter with "Dear Jim." If you call him "Mr. Wallace" in person, your salutation in correspondence is "Dear Mr. Wallace."

Q. *How does a married woman sign business correspondence?*
A. She signs with the name she uses in business, with no social title—that is, her first name with either her married name or her maiden name if she retained it for business after her marriage.

Q. *What is the proper way to use business cards? Are they ever used for social occasions?*
A. Business cards are never used for social purposes in the United States. They are limited to the use specified by their name: business. They are used in two main ways:

> When a business visit is made, a card is left as a record of the visit so that one's name, business firm, and phone number are readily available. It is not necessary to leave a card with subsequent visits to the same firm.

> When executives meet people with whom they want to keep in business contact they give them their card. This could take place at a business meeting or even at a cocktail party.

Business Entertaining

Q. *May I invite my boss to lunch?*
A. No, never. You may return an invitation to his or her home, because that becomes a social occasion, but you never return a business lunch or dinner invitation.

Q. *When a group of business associates gathers for lunch, who pays?*
A. The one who issues the invitation is considered the host and it is expected that he or she pay for the lunch. If, on the other hand, a group of business associates plans to have lunch so they can spend an out-of-the-office hour together, each generally pays for his or her own lunch.

Q. *How does a businessman or -woman know if a social invitation includes spouses or consorts?*
A. Usually the invitation is issued or addressed to both members of a couple. If, for some reason, you aren't sure if spouses are included, ask. If you are single, you should ask "shall I bring a date (or friend) or would you rather I came alone?" If you are living with someone, your companion should be treated exactly as a spouse would be. If your partner has been excluded from the invitation because of your host's

ignorance of the situation, all you need do is ask, "May I bring Susan Swanson, the woman I live with?" or "I live with Dave Ferris. Is it all right if I bring him?"

Q. *Whom should I invite to my daughter's wedding?*
A. If you are thinking of using your daughter's wedding to entertain clients, prospective clients, and business associates (and I hope you are not!), be careful not to slight anyone by failure to extend an invitation. Also be careful not to ruin your daughter's day by inviting a lot of people she does not know or does not care to know. If the wedding is small and personal you may invite only those business people whom you consider friends.

Q. *Whom should I invite to my son's bar mitzvah?*
A. The answer depends on the size of the celebration of the occasion, as it does with a wedding. If the bar mitzvah is small and intimate, you need invite only friends, some of whom may be business associates. If it is large, you may want to invite the entire office. You may even decide to omit business invitations to the religious service, extending them only to the party afterward.

Q. *What role does the spouse play in business entertaining?*
A. A spouse's role is to support you—to make your guests feel welcome, to help them enjoy being with you both, as well as to assist with refreshments. It is also your spouse's role to listen well, to ask questions

and to indicate the involvement of both of you in the company. Your spouse should feel free to discuss his or her profession and personal concerns, too, so long as the topic does not center on children and he or she does not monopolize the conversation.

Q. *My husband and I are returning the dinner invitation of his employer by giving a small dinner party in our home. How does my husband extend the invitation?*
A. The invitation should not be extended in person by your husband. Instead, you should write the invitation to your husband's boss and his or her spouse.

Q. *When giving a business dinner party at home without servants must both my husband and I greet guests at the door?*
A. Yes, whenever possible you both should be close by so introductions can be made and so one of you can take the guests' wraps while the other takes the guests around the room and introduces them to people they do not know.

Being Entertained at Home

Q. *What do you consider the hallmarks of a good guest? Of a good host and hostess?*
A. A good guest is enthusiastic, congenial, and considerate, treating other guests and the host and hostess, as well as their property, with thoughtfulness and respect. A good host and hostess are well prepared to see to the needs of each of their guests, having carefully planned for their comfort and entertainment.

Q. *The invitation says dinner at 7:30. What time should I arrive at the party?*
A. The answer depends on the custom in your area. If the custom is that guests are not expected to arrive until fifteen minutes to half an hour after the stated hour, it is wise to follow this practice.

Q. *When a party is given in someone's honor is he supposed to be the first guest to leave or the last?*
A. He is supposed to be the first to leave. This rule is more or less obsolete, however, so unless the guest of honor is the President of the United States, in which case no one may leave before he or she does, other guests may depart before the guest of honor.

Q. *Which is better—to send flowers to your hosts before or after a party?*

A. When a party is given especially for you, you should send flowers to your hostess beforehand. Otherwise, flowers sent later as a thank-you for a very special evening are always appreciated. Ordinarily, however, neither a gift sent later nor a note is necessary, and your verbal thanks when you leave is sufficient. A phone call the next day to say how much you enjoyed the evening is always welcome.

Q. *Should guests bring gifts of food or wine to their hosts?*

A. The custom of taking wine as a gift to a small dinner party is becoming customary. It is not too expensive or elaborate and has the advantage that if the hostess does not want to serve it that evening because she has planned another type of wine or a different beverage, she need not do so. She certainly may offer it, but no guest should feel insulted if his hostess says, ''Thanks so much! I already have wine planned for dinner, but we'll look forward to enjoying this another time!''

Gifts of food to be used for the dinner should never be taken unless the hostess has been consulted first. It is very disconcerting for a hostess who has planned a dessert to complement her meal to feel she must also serve another, unexpected dessert which may be too rich or uncomplementary. A box of candy, croissants and jam for the hosts' breakfast the next morning, or another gift of food given with the statement, "This is for you to enjoy tomorrow," resolves the problem.

If it is the custom in your area to take a gift to a small dinner party, by all means do so. For a large or formal party, however, it is better not to take a gift at all, especially if you do not know the hosts well. It may not be customary among their friends, and you will only embarrass your hostess and other guests who have not brought a gift. If you do know the hosts well and you have noticed that people generally do arrive with a gift, then follow the custom of the area.

Q. *How long should a hostess delay dinner for a late-arriving guest?*
A. Fifteen minutes is the established length of time. To wait more than twenty minutes, at the outside, would be showing rudeness to many for the sake of one. When the late guest finally arrives, he or she of course apologizes to the hostess and then is seated.

Q. *When a guest arrives late and we've already finished the first course, is that course served to the late-arriving guest?*
A. No, the latecomer is served whatever course is being eaten at the time he or she arrives, unless the course is dessert, in which case he or she would eat the entrée while others have their dessert.

Q. *How do the hosts politely end a party?*
A. The first and most effective way to end a party is

to close the bar. Offer "one last nightcap" and then—quite obviously—put the liquor away. The hostess may glance at her watch or hide a yawn. If these hints don't work, you can copy Peg Bracken's story about the kindly professor who said loudly to his wife, "Well, my dear, don't you think it's time we went to bed so these good people can go home?"

Q. *How long should a guest remain at a party, or in other words, how do I know to call it a night?*
A. Try to be sensitive and aware of the people around you. Most hostesses are reluctant to try to "speed the parting guest" so make an effort to observe when your hosts—and others at the party—begin to look tired, and make the move to break it up yourself. You should remain for at least one hour after dinner, as it is hardly complimentary to the hostess to "eat and run." At a small party you should not leave long before anyone else seems ready to go, because your departure is very apt to break up the party.

Q. *How do you take your leave at a large party? A small gathering?*
A. At a large party, locate your host and hostess, wait until they are free to speak to you for a moment, and thank them for a lovely evening. Insist that there is no need for them to see you to the door, find your coat or ask the maid, if there is one, and let yourself out.

At a small gathering, say your good-byes to the other guests, thank your host and hostess, find your wraps, and then depart. Nothing is more irritating than the guest who gets her coat, says good-bye to the other guests, and twenty minutes later is still standing in the open door talking with her hostess.

Q. *If everyone is having a good time would it be rude of the hosts to encourage their guests to remain longer?*
A. Not at all! It shows you are enjoying their company too, and if their offer to leave seems tentative, it is far friendlier to say, "Oh, don't go—it's Friday night and we can all sleep late tomorrow morning," than to jump up and bring them their coats the minute someone says, "Well, it's getting late . . ." If, however, they really must leave, one suggestion that they stay is enough. Don't force them to remain if they have a baby-sitter waiting or are firm in their resolve to go.

Q. *How can I discourage my guests from mixing their own drinks in my home?*
A. It is difficult to do without being insulting. You can control the situation somewhat, however, by going to the bar with your guest and asking them to get out the ice or the mix or whatever while you pour the liquor yourself. You can also avoid having more than one bottle of liquor in evidence if guests seem to be heavy drinkers, and you can make it obvious that you use a jigger to pour drinks and hand the jigger to your guests before they pour themselves.

Q. *How do I handle an inebriated guest?*

A. You must refuse to serve him or her more liquor. He or she may become insulted and abusive, but that is preferable to having him or her become more intoxicated. You are then responsible for seeing that a drunken guest is taken home by asking a good friend to take him or her, or you can go yourself if the distance isn't great, or you can call a cab, give the directions, and pay for it. The person's car keys should be taken away if he or she is not willing to be taken home by someone else. If your guest has reached the point of almost passing out, two or three other guests should help him or her to a bed to sleep it off overnight. If the inebriated person has a spouse or date present, you should offer this person accommodations too, or see that he or she gets home safely.

Q. *I got drunk at a party. Should I have called my hosts the next day and apologized?*

A. Yes, if your behavior was insulting or rude and if you disrupted the party you should apologize immediately. If you felt yourself getting drunk, however, and left the party without embarrassing yourself, the other guests, or your hosts, there is really little to apologize for except perhaps an early departure. You can mention this when you make your thank-you call by saying, "Your party was terrific! I'm sorry to have left a little early, but I had too much to drink and thought it was best to go before I passed out on your couch."

Q. *May I offer to help my hostess serve or clear the table?*

A. Yes, you may offer, but don't insist if she refuses your help. Most hostesses want you to relax or prefer to follow their own system of organization by themselves.

Invitations & Replies

Q. *What occasions call for formal third-person invitations? How is the invitation worded?*
A. The rule of thumb is that formal events require formal invitations. Occasions could include weddings, balls, formal dinner parties, dances, receptions, teas, commencements, bar and bat mitzvahs, and other official, state, or diplomatic parties.

The invitation is worded in the third person. For example:

Mr. and Mrs. Fernando Smith
request the pleasure of your company
at dinner
on Saturday, the fourth of July
at half past seven o'clock
Seabreeze
Edgartown, Massachusetts

R.s.v.p.
Box 636
Edgartown, Massachusetts 02539

Punctuation is used only when words requiring separation occur on the same line, and in certain abbreviations, such as "R.s.v.p." The time should never be given as "nine-thirty," but as "half past nine o'clock," or the more conservative form, "half after nine o'clock."

If the dance or dinner or other entertainment is to be given at one address and the hostess lives at another, both addresses are always given, assuming that the hostess wishes replies to go to her home address.

Q. *How far in advance of an occasion are invitations sent out?*
A. Depending on the type of occasion it is, invitations are usually sent between two and three weeks ahead of time, and they are to be answered at once. If a party is held at a catering hall or restaurant, however, the caterer often wants to know the number of guests attending at least two weeks before the party. If this is the case, invitations may be sent four weeks ahead. Wedding invitations are often sent up to five or six weeks ahead also, for the same reason.

Q. *How is the reply to a formal invitation worded when . . .*
. . . you are accepting the invitation?
A. The general rule is "reply-in-kind." The formal reply is written exactly as is the invitation, substituting the order of names. In accepting the invitation you must repeat the day and hour so that any mistake can be rectified. But if you decline an invitation it is not necessary to repeat the hour.

If the invitation reads:

> *Mr. and Mrs. Christopher Carvelas*
> *request the pleasure of your company*
> *at dinner*
> *on Saturday, the ninth of September*
> *at half past seven o'clock*
> *1411 Kenwood Parkway*
> *Miami Beach, Florida 33140*

R.s.v.p.

the acceptance reply would read:

> *Mr. and Mrs. Nicholas Maxwell*
> *accept with pleasure*
> *the kind invitation of*
> *Mr. and Mrs. Christopher Carvelas*
> *for dinner*
> *on Saturday, the ninth of September*
> *at half past seven o'clock*

Q. . . . *you must decline the invitation?*
A.

> *Mr. and Mrs. Nicholas Maxwell*
> *regret that they are unable to accept*
> *the kind invitation of*
> *Mr. and Mrs. Christopher Carvelas*
> *for Saturday, the ninth of September*

Q. *How is a wedding invitation worded?*

A. The following wording is correct for weddings of any size:

Mr. and Mrs. John Crosby

request the honour of your presence

at the marriage of their daughter

Catherine Elizabeth

to

Mr. Richard Drake O'Donnell

Saturday, the fifth of April

half after four o'clock

Church of St. John the Divine

Minneapolis

Q. *How are less formal invitations worded? How is the response worded?*

A. Less formal invitations may be a note, handwritten on an informal:

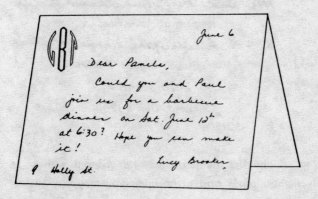

June 6

Dear Pamela,

Could you and Paul join us for a barbecue dinner on Sat. June 13ᵗ at 6:30? Hope you can make it!

Lucy Brooker

9 Holly St.

or they may be purchased, fill-in invitations:

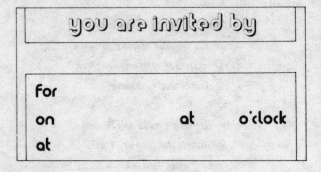

you are invited by

for

on   at   o'clock

at

or they may be printed with the printed lines following the wording of the formal, third-person invitation:

Mr. and Mrs. Arnold Davidson

request the pleasure of

Mr. and Mrs. Jonathan Field's

company at *dinner*

on *Saturday, the second of March*

at *eight o'clock*

44 High Street

Columbus, Ohio 43200

R.s.v.p.

The last invitation may be ordered with your
name already printed on it, or you may buy an un-

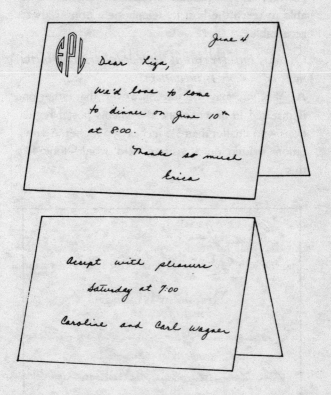

personalized set and fill in your own name.

The form of acceptance or regret depends upon the formality of the invitation received. If the R.s.v.p. information is a telephone number, then your response is called for. If it is not, a handwritten reply on your own informal or following the form of the printed, fill-in invitation is expected. If you are not able to reach the host by telephone a note is always acceptable.

Q. *May I use my visiting cards or informals as invitations or to reply to invitations?*
A. Yes, you may. Be sure, however, that either one is inserted in an envelope that meets postal regulations—no smaller than 3½ inches by 5 inches. An invitation written on a visiting card would look like this:

Wed. Jan. 8.
Bridge at 2. o'ck.

Mrs. John Kindhart

R. s. v. p.   1350 Madison Avenue

Q. *Is it acceptable to extend invitations by telephone?*
A. Yes. Telephone invitations are correct for all but the most formal dinners.

Q. *I've been invited to a cocktail buffet which is being held the weekend my cousin is visiting. May I ask my hostess if my cousin may attend?*

A. No. When regretting an invitation because you have a guest yourself, you should explain your reason to the hostess. She then has the option to say, "I'm sorry you can't come—we'll miss you!" or, if she feels the addition of your cousin won't make a difference in her planning, she may say, "Do bring him. I'd love to meet your cousin."

Q. *Can I change my response to an invitation . . .*
    . . . from yes to no?

A. Yes, but it is important that you call immediately, explain your problem, and express your regrets. If there is ample time, you may write, if you prefer, giving the reason and your apologies. In any event, it is essential that you let your hostess know right away.

Q. *. . . from no to yes?*

A. If the party to which you were originally invited is a large reception, a cocktail buffet, a picnic, or any gathering at which one or two more guests would not cause a complication, you may call the hostess, explain that circumstances have changed, and ask if you may change your regret to an acceptance. If, however, the party involves a limited number of guests, such as a seated dinner, a theater party, or bridge, the hostess will surely have filled your place and it would embarrass her if you asked to be reinstated.

Q. *What is a response card and how is it used?*

A. A response card, or answer card, is the least preferable form of obtaining a reply to an invitation, but it is acceptable. It is usually a small card that is engraved in the same style as the invitation it accompanies. Response cards have a place for the invited guest to check whether he or she will attend or not. It is not a good idea to have a fill-in space for "number that will attend" since some recipients assume this means they may bring additional guests. Answer cards with invitations to private parties usually include a self-addressed, stamped envelope.

Q. *I received a wedding invitation which included a response card. I am unable to attend the wedding. May I write a note explaining my regret at not being able to attend rather than return the response card?*

A. You should use the card for your reply. The sender has undoubtedly organized a system for filing the returned cards, and a handwritten answer on notepaper would not fit in with the cards. You may, however, accompany the card with a handwritten note explaining your regret, so long as it is included with the card, not in lieu of the card.

Q. *How soon after receiving an invitation should the guests respond?*

A. As soon as they know if they can accept or must regret the invitation.

Q. *If an invitation is addressed to Mr. and Mrs. does the invitation include their children?*

A. No, it does not. Only if the invitation was addressed "Mr. and Mrs. and family" or "and children" or if it listed the children's names after the adults' names are the children included in the invitation.

Q. *May an unmarried person bring a guest to a wedding?*
A. Of course, if his or her invitation reads "and guest." If it does not, then the invitation is intended only for the person to whom it is addressed.

Q. *When I receive a wedding invitation addressed to me "and guest" do I tell the bride and groom my guest's name when I respond?*
A. Yes, you should give her the name and address of your friend. Although it is not absolutely necessary, she should then send your guest an invitation.

Q. *How does a wedding announcement differ from an invitation?*
A. Announcements are just that—they announce that a wedding has taken place and they are sent after the wedding.

Q. *How is a wedding announcement worded? When are they sent? Who usually receives wedding announcements?*
A. It is never mandatory to send wedding announcements, but they are useful as a means of informing old friends who have been out of touch, business clients, people who live too far away to be able to attend, and closer friends who cannot be included when the wedding and reception lists are small. Announcements are never sent to anyone who has received an invitation

to the ceremony and/or the reception. Announcements are sent as soon after the wedding as possible, preferably the next day. If there is an extenuating circumstance they may, however, be mailed up to several months later.

A wedding announcement may be worded as follows:

> *Mr. and Mrs. Winthrop Hastings*
> *have the honour of*
> *announcing the marriage of their daughter*
> *Christine Nicole*
>
> *to*
>
> *Mr. Kenneth Kienzle*
> *Saturday, the twenty-seventh of March*
> *One thousand nine hundred and eighty-seven*
> *Washington, D.C.*

I feel, however, that it is especially nice if the family of the groom is included on the announcement with that of the bride, even though the bride's family pays for the announcements. This indicates an attitude of joining and the approval and joy the groom's family feels in the marriage:

Mr. and Mrs. Winthrop Hastings
and
Mr. and Mrs. Robert Kienzle
announce the marriage of
Christine Nicole Hastings
and
Kenneth Burns Kienzle
Saturday, the twenty-seventh of March
Trinity Church
New Milford, Connecticut

Q. *What obligation does a wedding announcement carry?*
A. None. As with an invitation to the wedding only, the receipt of an announcement does not demand a gift in return. Of course a gift may be sent, but it is not expected that you do so.

Celebrations

Q. *Which parents make the first call when their children get engaged?*

A. As soon as the prospective groom has talked with his parents, his mother should telephone the bride's mother, telling her how happy she is about the engagement and suggesting that they get together.

If the groom's parents do not realize they should make the initial move, the bride's parents should quickly do so. The only thing that's really important is that the families get together in a spirit of friendship.

Q. *Who announces the engagement at an engagement party?*

A. The conventional announcement is made by the father of the bride in the form of a toast. There are many simple but lovely toasts he may propose, such as, "Now you know that the reason for this party is to announce (bride's name)'s engagement to (groom's name). I would like to propose a toast to them both, wishing them many, many years of happiness."

Q. *Who is invited to an engagement party? Are gifts brought to and opened at an engagement party?*

A. The guest list is unlimited, but the majority of

engagement parties are restricted to relatives and good friends.

Engagement gifts are not expected from ordinary friends and acquaintances. They usually are given only by relatives and very special friends, and they generally are given to the bride alone. Sometimes they are given by the groom's family as a special welcome to the bride. Unless the custom in your family or your area is to bring gifts to the engagement party, in which case they are opened as part of the party, they should not be given at that time. It can cause embarrassment to those who have not brought anything. If guests do bring gifts, the bride should open them in private with only the donor present rather than making a display of them in front of those who did not bring anything.

Q. *How would a newspaper announcement of an engagement be worded?*

A. Each newspaper has its own special wording, and many have forms for you to complete from which they write the announcement themselves. Send your announcement to the society editor one to two weeks before it is to run. The date on which you would like the news to be published should be given to all papers so that the notices will appear simultaneously. The usual form for the announcement is as follows:

> Mr. and Mrs. Jacob Graham of Albany, New York, announce the engagement of their daughter, Frances [Mary Graham—*optional*], to Mr. Eugene Weiss, son of Mr. and

Mrs. Donald William Weiss of East Lansing, Michigan. A May wedding is planned.

Miss Graham was graduated from The State University of New York at Albany and is now Director of Special Education in Albany. Mr. Weiss was graduated from Michigan State University. He is at present associated with Highland Hotels in Albany.

Q. *Are engraved engagement announcements in good taste?*
A. No. You may, and should, however, send notes to or call relatives and close friends to inform them of your engagement before an engagement party or newspaper announcement. This prevents them from reading it first in the newspapers and consequently suffering hurt feelings.

Q. *How do guests dress for . . .*
. . . a formal daytime wedding?
A. Women guests should wear street-length afternoon or cocktail dresses. Colors are preferable to black or white. Gloves should be worn, and head coverings are optional.

Men should wear dark suits, conservative shirts, and ties.

Q. *. . . a formal evening wedding?*
A. Women guests, depending on local custom, should wear long or short dresses. Head coverings and gloves are optional.

If women wear long dresses, men should wear

tuxedos. If women wear short dresses, men may wear tuxedos or dark suits.

Q. . . . *a semiformal daytime wedding?*
A. Women guests wear short afternoon or cocktail dresses.

Men should wear dark suits, conservative shirts, and a tie.

Q. . . . *a semiformal evening wedding?*
A. Women guests may wear cocktail dresses, gloves, and a small hat or a veil.

Men guests wear dark suits, conservative shirts, and a tie.

Q. . . . *an informal daytime wedding?*
A. Women guests wear afternoon dresses and gloves. A head covering for church is optional.

Men guests wear dark suits or light trousers and dark blazers in summer.

Q. . . . *an informal evening wedding?*
A. Women guests wear afternoon or cocktail dresses, gloves, and a head covering for church if they wish.

Men guests wear dark suits, conservative shirts, and a tie.

Q. *Are wedding presents addressed to the bride alone, or to both the bride and groom?*
A. A wedding present given before the wedding is addressed to the bride alone. A gift given after the wedding is addressed to both the bride and the groom.

Q. *When and where are wedding gifts delivered? Are gifts brought to a wedding reception?*

A. Gifts are generally delivered to the bride's home before the day of the wedding. They may be delivered in person or they may be sent directly from the store where they were purchased.

In some localities and among certain ethnic groups it is customary to take your gift to the wedding reception rather than send it ahead of time. Checks are usually handed to the bride and groom as you go through the receiving line, but gift packages are placed on a table prepared for them, as soon as you arrive. If there is a large number of presents, the bride and groom do not open them until a later date, so that they will have time to enjoy the other festivities. If there are only a few, however, they should open them after the receiving line breaks up. One of the bride's attendants should help, disposing of wrappings and keeping a careful list of the gifts.

Q. *Who writes the thank-you notes, the bride or the groom? How are they signed, with only the bride's or groom's name, or with both names?*

A. Since most gifts are sent to the bride, she usually writes and signs the thank-you note, but there is no reason the groom should not share this task. There are many relatives and friends of the groom who would be delighted to receive a thank-you note from him.

It is not incorrect to sign both names, but it is preferable to sign only one name and include the

other in the text: "Bob and I are so delighted with
. . . , etc." or "Jean and I . . . , etc."

Q. *Traditionally, which side of the aisle does the
bride's family sit on?*
A. The left side.

Q. *Where do the divorced parents of the bride (or
groom) sit in church? at the reception?*
A. If the parents have remained on friendly terms,
the mother and stepfather sit in the front pew with
members of the mother's immediate family—grandparents, aunts, and uncles—immediately behind them.
The father sits in the next pew back with his wife and
their family members.

If the parents have not remained on friendly
terms but the bride (or groom) is close to both of them
it is more difficult. The seating arrangement is the
same unless the bride (or groom) has been living with
the father and stepmother and have had little to do
with the mother. In this case, the father and stepmother sit in the front pew.

Divorced parents of the bride or groom are never
seated together at the parents' table at the reception.
If they are reasonably friendly, the parent giving the
reception will invite the other, but will seat him or her
at a separate table.

Q. *What is the traditional division of expenses between the bride's and groom's families?*
A. The bride's family traditionally pays the following
expenses:

- The invitations and announcements
- The bride's wedding dress and accessories
- The service of a bridal consultant, if desired
- Floral decorations for the church and the reception
- Bouquets for the bridesmaids
- Bouquet for the bride (unless local custom is that it is provided by the groom)
- Corsages for the bride's mother and grandmothers, unless the groom is providing them
- Boutonniere for the bride's father
- Music for the church and the reception
- The church sexton's fee
- Transportation for the bridal party to the church and then to the reception, if rented limousines are used
- All the expenses of the reception
- Bride's presents to her attendants
- Bride's present to her groom if she wishes to give him one
- Groom's wedding ring
- Hotel accommodations for the bride's attendants if they cannot stay with friends, neighbors, or relatives
- Travel expenses and hotel accommodations for the clergyman if he has been invited by the bride's family and must travel a distance to perform the ceremony
- Formal wedding photographs and candid pictures

- Awnings, a tent for an outdoor reception, and ribbons and a carpet for the church aisle if not provided by the church
- The services of a traffic policeman, if necessary.

The groom's family traditionally pays the following expenses:

- Bride's engagement and wedding rings
- Groom's present to his bride, if he wishes to give her one
- Gifts for the best man and the ushers
- Hotel accommodations for the groom's attendants if they can't stay with friends, neighbors, or relatives
- Ties, gloves, and boutonnieres for the best man and ushers
- The groom's and his father's boutonnieres
- The clergyman's fee or donation
- The marriage license
- Transportation for the groom and his best man to the church
- Expenses of the honeymoon
- The rehearsal dinner
- The bride's bouquet in areas where it is the custom
- The bride's going-away corsage
- Corsages for immediate members of both families, unless the bride has included them in her florist's order

- Bachelor dinner, if he wishes to give one
- Groom's parents pay their own transportation and lodging expenses
- Travel expenses and hotel accommodations for the clergyman if he has been invited by the groom's family and must travel a distance to perform the ceremony

Q. *How can a bride make it known she'll be using her own name after the wedding? Can she include a small card with the invitation?*
A. An addition to the end of the wedding announcement for the newspaper reading, "Miss Harris plans to retain her maiden name," is a good way to make it known. A card included with the invitation is not appropriate, but "at home" cards included with announcements sent after the wedding clearly impart the information:

Emily Jean Harris
and
Theodore Coyne Bridges
at home after the third of November
[etc.]

Q. *Are there any rules about who can and cannot host a bridal or baby shower?*
A. Almost anyone who wants to may give a shower. The one rule is that immediate family—meaning mothers, mothers-in-law, and sisters—should not, under ordinary circumstances, give showers.

Q. *We are having our first baby soon and want to send birth announcements but are fearful people will think they are a bid for gifts. Do birth announcements obligate the receivers to send a gift?*

A. No. Birth announcements carry no obligation. They do not mean that the recipients need send gifts. It is thoughtful, however, for those who receive announcements to send a note of congratulations to the new parents.

Q. *Is there a standard form for birth announcement cards? Are birth announcements sent to local newspapers? If so, how would one be worded?*

A. No, there is no standard form. There is a large variety of commercially designed announcement cards available, as well as a large selection of announcements available through printers. Often parents design their own announcements, which can be the nicest cards of all. Another one of the nicest types of birth announcements consists simply of a very small card with space for the baby's name and birth date on it, tied with a pink or blue ribbon to the top of the "Mr. and Mrs." card of the parents.

Birth announcements may be sent to newspapers in the week following the birth: "Mr. and Mrs. Steven Krieger of 114 Keystone Avenue, Columbus, announce the birth of a son, Benjamin, on July 2, 1987, at Doctor's Hospital. They have one daughter, Beth, three. Mrs. Krieger is the former Miss Barbara Dillon."

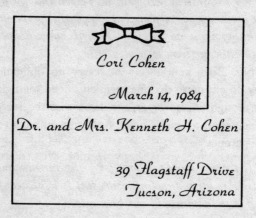

Cori Cohen

March 14, 1984

Dr. and Mrs. Kenneth H. Cohen

39 Flagstaff Drive
Tucson, Arizona

Birth announcement

Q. *May we send birth announcements when we adopt a child?*

A. Most certainly. An announcement for an adopted child will bring reassuring comfort to the child later on, should he or she ever doubt his place in the hearts of the family who chose him.

> *Mr. and Mrs. Michael Teppert*
> *have the happiness to announce*
> *the adoption of*
> *Sarah*
> *age four months*

Or if announcements are sent during the legal proceedings, the wording may be changed:

Mr. and Mrs. Michael Teppert
have the happiness to announce
the arrival of
Sarah
June twelfth, 1987
age one month

If you choose to use a commercial birth announcement for your adopted child, choose one in which you can easily insert the words *adopted* or *adoption* and one appropriate to the child's age. In other words, don't select a card with a picture of a stork with a baby in its mouth to announce the arrival of a two-year-old. If you prefer to design your own card, one of the nicest I've seen was the card sent by a family who already had a son and a daughter, shown on page 146.

Q. *Are written thank-you notes necessary for gifts friends brought to the hospital when my baby was born?*
A. No, if you give warm thanks at the time, you need not then write a note. However, when gifts are sent, a note—or a phone call, to close friends—is in order. The note may be written on an informal or on a thank-you card with a personal message. It should be signed with the mother's name, not the baby's.

Q. *How are invitations to a christening or* brit *issued?*
A. Usually, christening invitations are given over the telephone—or to out-of-towners, by personal note:

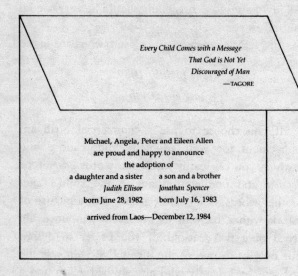

*Every Child Comes with a Message
That God is Not Yet
Discouraged of Man*
—TAGORE

Michael, Angela, Peter and Eileen Allen
are proud and happy to announce
the adoption of

a daughter and a sister	a son and a brother
Judith Ellisor	*Jonathan Spencer*
born June 28, 1982	born July 16, 1983

arrived from Laos—December 12, 1984

Adoption announcement

> *Dear Annemarie and George,*
> *Julie will be christened on Sunday, the 23rd, at*
> *3:00 in Christ Church. Would you come to the*
> *ceremony at the church, and join us afterward at*
> *our house?*
>
> > *Love,*
> > *Allison*

Or a message may be written on the "Mr. and Mrs." cards of the parents or on an informal, saying simply, "Julie's christening, Christ Church, March

23rd, 3 o'clock. Reception at our house afterward."
All invitations to a christening should be very friendly
and informal.

For a *brit,* relatives and close friends are invited
by telephone since the time between birth and the
ceremony is short.

Q. *How should godparents be chosen?*
A. One must never ask any but a most intimate friend
or relative to be a godparent, for it is a responsibility
not to be undertaken lightly and also one difficult to
refuse.

Q. *What are the obligations of a godparent toward
their godchild?*
A. The obligation of being a godparent is essentially
a spiritual one which recommends that the godparent be of the same faith as the parents. The godparent vows to see that the child is given religious
training, learns the specific creeds and command-
ments of the church, and is confirmed at the proper
time.

Beyond these obligations he is expected to take
a special interest in the child, much as a very close
relative would do, remembering him or her with a gift
on birthdays and on Christmas until the child is grown
—or perhaps longer if they remain close.

Godparents who have lost contact with the child
and his or her parents need not continue to give presents after the threads of friendship have broken.

Godparents do not have any obligation to give
financial assistance or to assume the care of children

who lose their parents. This responsibility is the guardian's—not the godparents.

Q. *Who provides the christening outfit, the parents or the godparents?*
A. The parents do. The dress may be new, or is often one that was worn by the baby's mother, father, or even one of his or her grandparents or great-grandparents. Usually everything the baby wears is white, although this is a custom, not a church requirement.

Q. *Who hosts an anniversary party? May the couple host the party or do family members plan the party?*
A. Early anniversary parties are always given by the couple themselves. By the time they reach the twenty-fifth they may well have grown children who wish to make the arrangements, but it is perfectly correct for them to do so themselves if the young people do not or cannot. When a couple do not have children, close friends sometimes prepare the celebration. Fiftieth-anniversary celebrations are almost invariably planned by the family of the couple.

Q. *How are invitations chosen for an anniversary party?*
A. The form of the invitations depends entirely on the degree of formality of the party. They may range from an informal telephone call to an engraved third-person invitation. Formal invitations for a twenty-fifth anniversary are often bordered and printed in silver; those for a fiftieth, in gold. The most common forms

are handwritten notes, or the necessary information written on an informal or a fill-in card.

Q. *Are gifts brought to an anniversary party? Are they opened at the party or privately after the party?*
A. If the invitation includes a line reading "no gifts, please," no gifts should be taken to the party. If that line does not appear, gifts should be taken to the party. In this case, the opening of the packages is a feature of the party. After everyone has arrived, or perhaps after dinner while the guests are enjoying their coffee, everyone gathers around and the couple open the gifts and thank the donors. One of their children, or anyone they choose to designate, helps by taking care of the wrappings, making a list, etc. The couple do not need to write notes later to those they have already thanked, unless they wish to do so.

Index

Acceptance of invitations:
  after declining, 129
  formal, 123–25
  less formal, 127
Acknowledgment of gift,
  lack of, 81–84
Address, forms of, 4–7
  in business situations, 110
  for telephone calls, 60–
  61; business calls, 63
  for waiters, 44–48
Addressing of wedding
  presents, 137
Adoption of child,
  announcement of,
  144–45
Advance time for
  invitations, 123
Affection, public displays,
  13, 16
Age, questions about, 80
Airline personnel, tips, 99
A la carte, 45–46
Animals. *See* Pets
Anniversary parties,
  148–49
Announcements:
  of adoption of child,
  144–45

Announcements *(cont.)*
  of birth of child, 143–45
  of engagement, 134–36
  of wedding, 131–33
Answer cards, 130
Answering of telephone,
  60
Answering services, 104
Apartment living, 14–15
Arrival time, at dinner
  parties, 115
  late for dinner, 117
At home cards, 142

Baby gifts, thank-you
  notes, 145
Baby shower, 142
Baby-sitter, tips for, 104
Bachelor dinner expense,
  142
Bar car waiter, tip for, 102
Bar mitzvah invitations,
  113
Bar steward, tip for, 100
Barber, tip for, 104
Bartender, tip for, 95
Bath steward, tip for, 100
Beach behavior, 15–16
Beauty salon, tips, 105

Beginning of meal, 28, 29
Bellman, tip for, 100
Beverages:
  hot, 39–40
  iced, 40
  See also Glasses
Birth announcements,
  143–45
Blind people, behavior
  with, 56
Blowing of nose at table, 41
Boss, inviting of, 112, 114
Bracken, Peg, 118
Bread:
  and butter, to eat, 38
  uncut, in restaurant,
  46–47
Bread-and-butter plate. *See*
  Butter plate
Bridal consultant, 140
Bridal showers, hosts, 142
Bride:
  divorced parents at
    wedding, 139
  engagement gifts, 135
  family of, wedding
    expenses, 139–41
Bridegroom:
  gift from bride, 140
  and wedding gift
    thank-you notes,
    138–39
Bridegroom, family of:
  duplicate wedding gifts
    from, 93
  expenses of wedding,
    141–42
  and wedding
    announcements,
    132–33

Bridesmaids' expenses, 140
Brit. invitation to, 147
Broken gifts, 92
Building employees, tips
  for, 108–9
Burial, attendance, 75
Busboy, tip for, 52, 95
Bus driver, tip for, 99
Business associates:
  first-name use, 3
  funerals, 77
  and living-together
    relationship, 88
Business cards, 111
Business entertaining,
  112–14
  thank-yous, 85
Business letters:
  salutations, 110–11
  signature of married
    woman, 111
Business situations:
  names and titles, 110–11
  reception of clients,
    10–11
  telephone manners,
    63–64
Butchers, tips for, 105
Butter knife, table setting:
  family-style, 27
  formal, 22
  informal, 25
Butter plate, 33
  family-style setting, 27
  formal table setting, 20
  informal table setting, 24

Cabin boys, tips for, 100
Cabin stewards, tips for,
  99

Cafeterias, 51–52
  tips for busboys, 95
Caller on telephone,
    identification of, 60–61
Calling cards, 84–87
  for invitations, 128
Candles, table settings, 23
Car door, opening of, 12
Caterers, tips for, 95–96
Chambermaid, tip for, 101
Champagne, serving of, 30
  glasses for, 31
Changes:
  of place of worship,
    66–67
  in response to invitation,
    129
Checkroom, at restaurant,
    43
  tip for attendant, 96
Child care, tips for, 104
Children:
  adoption announcement,
    144–45
  and adults-only visit, 57
  barbers of, tips for, 104
  dress for funeral, 75
  hand shakes, 10
  inclusion in invitations,
    130–31
  introduction of parents,
    4
  offering of seat, 12–13
  rising for guests, 11
  visit from, 57–58
Chinese restaurants, 52
Choking on food, 41
Christening clothes, 148
Christening invitations,
    145–47

Church:
  changing of, 66–67
  expenses for wedding,
    140
Church services, 65–67
Cigarette smoking, 14
Claret glasses, 31
Cleaners, tips for, 105
Clear soups, 37–38
Clergy for wedding,
    expenses of, 140, 141,
    142
Clothing:
  beach wear, 16
  christening outfit, 148
  for funerals, 74–75
  for weddings, 136–37
  for worship services, 65
Club car waiters, tips, 102
Club personnel, tips for,
    95, 103
Coat, checked at
    restaurant, 43
Cocktails, 46
Coffee service:
  family-style table setting,
    28
  with informal meal, 26
  in restaurant, 47
Coffee spoon, table setting,
    26
Color, in table settings, 23
Communication,
    interpersonal, 79–89
Complaints about
    restaurant service,
    49–50
Condiments, service of, 33
  family-style meals, 26
Condolence calls, 68

Condolence cards, printed, 76
Condolence notes, 73, 80
  thank-yous for, 82
Congratulations, thank-you notes for, 82, 83
Contributions, in lieu of flowers, 71
Conversations:
  when newly introduced, 9
  with strangers, 79–80
Correspondence, to couple with different names, 6
Corsages, wedding, 140, 141
Cost, questions about, 80
Coughing, at table, 41
Couples:
  anniversary parties, 148
  with different names, 6
  walking together, 11–12, 13
Cruise directors, 100
Cruise ship personnel, tips for, 99–100
Cup, table setting:
  family-style, 28
  informal, 26

Dairy deliverers, tips, 105
Damaged gifts, 92
Daughter's wedding, invitations to business associates, 113
Daytime weddings, dress for, 136, 137
Deaf people, behavior with, 54–55
Deaths:
  condolence calls, 68–69

Deaths (cont.)
  newspaper notices, 69–71
  notification of relatives, 69
Declining of invitation:
  after acceptance, 129
  formal, 123–24
  less formal, 127
Delivery of wedding gift, 138
Delivery people, tips, 105–8
Departure from party, 115, 118–19
Desk clerk, tip for, 101
Dessert, 35–36
  how to eat, 37
Dessert fork, table setting, 23
Dessert spoon, 35–36
  family-style setting, 27
  formal table setting, 23
  informal table setting, 25
Diaper service, tips, 106
Dining car waiter, tips, 102
Dining steward, tips for, 99
Dinner fork, table setting, 27
Dinner guest:
  refusal of dish, 34
  request for missing item, 33
Dinner invitation to boss, 112
Dinner knife, table setting:
  family-style, 27
  informal, 24

Dinner party:
  for business associates, 114
  ending of meal, 29
  gift to host, 116–17
  late-arriving guest, 117
  thank-you note, 82, 83
  time of arrival, 115
  tips for waiters, 97
  See also Formal dinner
Dinner plate, table setting:
  family-style, 27
  informal, 23, 25–26
Dirty silver, in restaurant, 19
Disabled people, behavior with, 54–56
Divorce, announcement of, 89
Divorced persons:
  and funeral of ex-spouse, 74
  parents of bride, at wedding, 139
  woman, form of name, 7
Doggy bags, 49
Doorman, tip for, 101, 108
Dress:
  beach wear, 16
  of bride, expense of, 140
  for christening, 148
  for formal wedding, 136–37
  for funeral, 74–75
  for worship service, 65
Drinks. *See* Beverages
Drunken guests, 120
Duplicate gifts, exchange of, 93

Elevator operator, tips, 109
Elevators, 13
Employer, invitations to, 112, 114
Ending of meal, formal, 29
Engagement:
  announcement of, 134–36
  broken, gifts returned, 92
  visits by parents, 134
Engagement party, 134–35
Engagement ring, 141
England, tipping in, 109
Entertaining:
  at home, 115–21;
    business associates, 114
  for business, 112–14
Escalators, 12
Ethnic groups, money gifts, 90
Ethnic slurs, 53–54
Europe:
  tipping in, 109
  use of flatware, 35
Evening weddings, dress for, 136–37
Exchange of gifts, 93
Ex-family members, introduction of, 5

Family members, introductions, 2, 3–4
Family of bride:
  and engagement, 134
  wedding expenses, 139–41
Family of groom, wedding expenses, 141–42
Family-style dining, 19–20
  service of food, 33–34
  table settings, 26–28

Father of bride, engagement announcement, 134
Fiftieth anniversary, 148
  gifts, 90
Fill-in invitations, 126–27
First names, 3
  in business situation, 110
  of parents, 4
Fish fork, table setting, 21
Fish knife, table setting, 22
Flatware:
  dirty, in restaurants, 19
  for family-style meals, 26
  order of use, 34
  See also Forks; Knives; Spoons; Table settings
Flight attendants, 99
Florist, tip for, 106
Flowers:
  at deaths, 72
  for hostess, 116
  for memorial service, 75
  for wedding, 140, 141
Food:
  choking on, 41
  excess, in restaurants, 49
  family-style service, 28, 33–34
  foreign objects in, 41–42
  gift to host, 116–17
  removal from mouth, 40
  spilled, 42
  stuck in tooth, 42
  wrapped, in restaurant, 47
Foreign object in food, 41–42
Forgotten name, in introduction, 8

Forks:
  family-style setting, 27
  formal table setting, 21, 23
  informal table setting, 23
  proper use, 34–35
Formal dinner:
  spills, 42
  table settings, 20–23
  use of napkin, 28–29
  See also Dinner party
Formal invitations, 122–23
  responses 123–25
Formal wedding, dress for, 136–37
Frozen dinners, 26
Fruit, eating of, 37
  in cocktails, 46
Fruit spoon, table setting, 22
Funeral:
  attendance, 74, 77
  flowers, 71–72
  ushers, 77–78
Funeral home visits, 68–69, 73, 74, 76
Furniture movers, tips, 107

Garage valet, tips for, 101
Garbage collector, tips, 106
Gift certificates, 90
Gifts, 90–93
  at anniversary party, 149
  baby gifts, 145
  from bride, 140
  for engagements, 135
  to godchildren, 147
  from groom, 141
  from guest after visit, 84

Gifts *(cont.)*
  to hosts, 116–17
  questions about cost, 80
  thank-you notes, 82, 83
  unacknowledged, 81–84
  and wedding
    announcements, 133
  wedding presents, 137–38
Glasses, table settings:
  family-style, 27
  formal, 21
  informal, 25
Godparents, 147–48
Golf caddy, tip for, 103
Good manners, ix–x
Good neighbors, 53
Grace at meals, 28
Gravy, 33
Greetings:
  before worship service, 66
  in restaurant, 48–49
Grief, times of, 68–78
Grocery loader, tips, 106
Groom. *See* Bridegroom
Guardians, responsibilities
    of, 148
Guest of honor, when to
    leave party, 115
Guests:
  drunken, 120
  good, 115
  host gift, after visit, 84
  late for dinner party, 117
  rising to greet, 11
  unexpected, 58–59
Guide dog, 56

Hair, arrangement of, in
    restaurants, 48
Hairdresser, tip for, 104–5

Handicapped people,
    behavior with, 54–56
Hand shakes, 9–10
  rising for, 11
Handwritten invitations,
    125–28
  response to, 127–28
Handymen, tips for, 108
Hats:
  in restaurant, 43
  in worship service, 65
Headwaiter, tip for,
    50–51, 95, 96, 102
Hearing aids, 55
Help, at times of death,
    68, 72–73
Home entertainment,
    115–21
  business associates, 114
Honeymoon expenses, 141
Honorary pallbearers, 73,
    77
Hospital:
  gifts for staff, 106
  smoking rules, 14
  visits, 57
Host:
  of anniversary party, 148
  ending of party, 117–18
  good, 115
  of restaurant dinner,
    50–51
  rising for guests, 11
  of shower, 142
  See also Hostess
Hostess:
  beginning of meal, 28
  ending of meal, 29
  flowers for, 116
  offer of assistance to, 121

Hotels:
European, tipping in, 109
tips for personnel,
100–102, 107
wedding party
accommodations, 140,
141
Hot food, 40
beverages, 39–40
bread, buttering of, 38
when to eat, 29
Household help, tips for,
104, 107
Houses of worship, 65–67
Husband-and-wife calling
cards, 85, 87

Ice cream, 37
Iced beverages, 40
Identification of telephone
caller, 60–61, 63–64
Incorrect introductions, 9
Informal meal:
spills, 42
table setting, 20, 23–28
See also Semiformal meals
Informal notes, 128
Informal wedding, dress
for, 137
In lieu of flowers, 71–
72
Instructor, tip for, 103
Introductions, 1–5
forgotten name, 8
hand shakes, 9–10
incorrect, 9
of live-in partners, 88
response to, 8–9
in restaurants, 48
rising for, 10–11

Invitations, 80–81, 122–33
anniversary party, 148–
49
to business associates,
112–13, 114
christening, 145–46
by telephone, 61–62

Janitors, tips for, 108
Japanese restaurants, 52
Jars, food served in, 26
Jelly, in restaurants, 47
Jewish families, condolence
calls, 68
Joint calling cards, 85, 87

Knives:
family-style setting, 27
formal table setting,
21–23
informal table setting,
24–25
proper use, 34–35

"Ladies first" rule, 12
Large party, departure
from, 118
Late-arriving guests, 117
Laundry service, tips, 107
Leaving of parties, 118–19
Legal signature of married
woman, 6
Letter carrier, tip for, 107
Linens, table settings, 22
Lipstick, use of, 19, 48
Liquor, control at party,
119–20
Live-in partners, 87–88
introduction of, 4, 88
and invitations, 112–13

Live-in servants, tips for, 104, 107
Locker-room attendant, 103
Loss, times of, 68–78
Lounge stewards, tips, 100
Lunch, business, 112
Lunch counter tips, 97

Maiden name, used after marriage, 6, 142
Mailman, tip for, 107
Manicurist, tip for, 104
Manners, changes in, ix–x
Marmalade, in restaurant, 47
Marriage license, 141
Married women, names, 6–7
Masseur, tips for, 103
Meat fork, table setting, 21
Meat knife, table setting, 22
Memorial service, 75–76
ushers, 77–78
Men:
 dress for weddings, 136–37
 hand shakes, 9–10
 introduced to women, 1
 walking with women, 11–12
Menus, in restaurants, 45–46
Messenger, tip for, 105
Milkman, tip for, 105
Minority groups, and ethnic slurs, 53–54
Money gifts, 91
 wedding presents, 90, 138

Motel personnel, 100–102
Mother of bride, and engagement, 134
Movers, tips for, 107
Mugs, for hot beverages, 39
Music, for wedding, 140
Musicians, tips for, 97

Names, 4–7
 business situation, 110–11
 changes of, 7–8
 in death notices, 70
 forgetting of, 8
 in introductions, 2–3
 maiden name, used after marriage, 6, 142
 suffixes, 7
 of telephone caller, 60–61
Napkin rings, 26
Napkins, 28–29
 family-style meals, 26, 27–28
 formal table setting, 22
 informal table setting, 25
Neighborliness, 53
Newlyweds, name for spouses' parents, 5
Newspaper carrier, tip for, 108
Newspaper announcements:
 of birth, 143
 death notices, 69–71
 of engagement, 135–36
Nose, blowing, at table, 41
No-smoking rules, 14
Nurses, gifts for, 106

Obituaries, 71
Obligations of godparents,
147–48
Obligatory thank-you notes,
82, 84
Obscene telephone calls,
62–63
Offensive forms of address,
110
Older person:
first-name use, 3
young person introduced,
1
Optional thank-you notes,
83, 85
Ordering of food, in
restaurant, 44–45
Oriental restaurants, 52
Overnight visit, thank-you
note, 82
Oyster fork, table settings,
22, 27

Pallbearers, 73
Paper napkins, 26
Parents:
of bride, divorced, 139
engagement of child,
134
of friends, names for, 5
introduction of, 4
Parking of car, 101, 108
Parks, behavior in, 16
Parties:
control of liquor, 119–20
departure from, 115,
118–19
ending of, 117–18
Personal letters, 80–81
Personal questions, 80

Pets:
objection to, 16–17
taken on visits, 59
Photographs of wedding,
140
Pie, eating of, 37
Playgrounds, behavior in,
16
Porters, tips for, 99, 100
on trains, 102
Posture at dinner table, 20
Prejudices, social, 80
President of United States,
leaving of party, 115
Printed cards to
acknowledge sympathy
expressions, 76–77
Printed invitations, 126–27
Professional people, form
of address, 3, 7
Public behavior, 15–16
arrangement of hair, 48
displays of affection, 13
smoking rules, 14
Public transportation,
seating, 12–13

Rank:
and first-name use, 3
and hand shakes, 10
and introductions, 2
Reaching, at table, 33
Red wine, serving of,
29–30
glasses for, 31
Regrets. See Declining of
invitation
Rehearsal dinner, 141
Reservation at restaurant,
42–43

Residential building
  employees, tips for,
  108–9
Residential hotel personnel,
  tips for, 107
Response to introduction,
  8–9
Response to invitation:
 answer cards, 130
 change of, 129
 formal, 123–25
 telephone, 61–62
Restaurants, 42–52
 European, tipping in, 109
 greetings in, 11
 tip for headwaiter, 95, 96
Revolving doors, 12
Rising to feet, 10–11
 in restaurant, 48–49
Room waiter, tip for, 102

Salad, how to eat, 39
Salad bowls, 26
Salad fork, table settings,
  21, 23
Salad knife, table setting,
  21
Salad plate, 23, 27
Salt, use of, 40
Salutation of letter,
  110–11
Sarnoff, Dorothy, 79
Seat, giving up of, 12–13
Seating:
 in cafeterias, 52
 at funerals, 77–78
 in restaurants, 43–44
 at weddings, 139
 in worship services,
  65–66

Self, introduction of, 3
Semiformal invitations,
  125–28
Semiformal meals, 23–26
Semiformal weddings,
  dress for, 137
Servants, dinner party
  without, 114
Service of food,
  family-style, 33–34
Service plates, 20, 25
Shaking hands, 9–10
 rising for, 11
Sherry, serving of, 29
Ship's officers, 100
Shoeshines, tips for, 109
Shower, host of, 142
Shower gifts:
 and broken engagement,
  92
 thank-you notes, 82, 83
Sick person:
 thank-you note from, 82
 visit to, 57
Side dish, in restaurant, 46
Signatures:
 of wedding gift thank-you
  notes, 138–39
 of women, 111; married
  women, 6
Silver. See Flatware
Sitting, at dinner table, 20
Sitting shivah, 68
Skycap, tips for, 99
Sleeping car porter, 102
Small party, departure
  from, 118–19
Smoking, 14
Smorgasbord restaurants,
  51

Toasts, engagement
announcement, 134
Tooth, food stuck in, 42
Tour guides, tips for, 99
Train personnel, tips, 102
Travel expenses, for
wedding clergy, 140,
142
Twenty-fifth anniversary
party, 148
Typing of personal letters,
80–81

Unacknowledged gifts, 81,
84
Unexpected gifts, 91
Unexpected guests, 58–59
Unmarried couples:
address of
correspondence, 6
communication of
relationship, 87–88
introduction of partner, 4
and invitations, 112–13;
wedding invitations,
131
Unnecessary thank-you
notes, 83, 85
Unsatisfactory service,
tipping, 50, 94
Ushers:
in church, 65–66
at funerals, 77–78
tips for, 109

Valets, in hotels, 102
Visiting cards, 84–86
for invitations, 128
Visitors, included in
invitations, 129

Visits:
from children, 57–58
of condolence, 68–69; at
funeral home, 73, 74
to hospitals, 57
overnight, thank-yous, 82
pets and, 59
unexpected guests, 58–59

Waiter:
to summon, 47–48
tips for, 97
tipping, hotel dining
room, 101
tipping, on trains, 102
Walking, in couples,
11–12
Washroom attendant, 98
Water goblet, 31
informal table setting, 25
Wedding announcement,
131–33
expense of, 140
at home card, 142
Wedding attendants,
expenses of, 141
Wedding dress, 140
Wedding gifts, 92, 137
acknowledgment of, 93
duplicate, exchange of, 93
money as, 90
thank-you notes, 84
Wedding invitations, 125
advance time, 123
to business associate,
113
expenses of, 140
to guests of unmarried
persons, 131
response cards, 130

Wedding reception, 140,
    141
  seating of divorced
    parents, 139
Wedding rings, 140, 141
Weddings:
  dress of guests, 136–37
  expenses of, 139–42
White wine, serving of, 29
  glasses for, 31
Widows, form of name,
    6–7
Wine:
  host gifts, 116
  serving of, 29–31
Wineglasses, 29–31
  table settings, 21, 25
Wine stewards, tips for, 98
  on cruise ships, 100
Women:
  in business, reception of
    clients, 10–11
  dress for formal
    weddings, 136
  dress for informal
    weddings, 137

Women (cont.)
  dress for semiformal
    weddings, 137
  hand shakes, 9, 10
  legal signatures, 111
  men introduced to, 1
  names in death notices,
    70
  ordering in restaurant,
    44–45
  professional, form of
    address, 7
  rising to feet, 11
  seating in church, 66
  signatures of, 6–7
  walking with men, 11–
    12
Worship services, 65–67
  smoking rules, 14
Wrapped food, in
    restaurant, 47
Wrong telephone numbers,
    62

Young person, introduced
    to older person, 1

About the Author

Elizabeth L. Post, granddaughter-in-law of the legendary Emily Post, has earned the mantle of her predecessor as America's foremost authority on etiquette. Mrs. Post has revised the classic *Etiquette* since 1965, and has written *Emily Post's Complete Book of Wedding Etiquette, Emily Post's Wedding Planner, Please, Say Please, The Complete Book of Entertaining* with co-author Anthony Staffieri, and *Emily Post Talks with Teens About Manners and Etiquette* with co-author Joan M. Coles. Mrs. Post's advice on etiquette may also be found in the monthly column she writes for *Good Housekeeping* magazine, "Etiquette for Everyday."

Mrs. Post and her husband divide their time between homes in Vermont and Florida.